FORENSIC IDENTIFICATION
Putting a Name and Face on Death

ELIZABETH A. MURRAY

Twenty-First Century Books
Minneapolis

ACKNOWLEDGMENTS AND DEDICATION: I extend sincere thanks to my sister, Kathleen Isaacs, and my friend, Elizabeth Villing, for reviewing an early draft of this work. This book acknowledges all those who work tirelessly in the effort to put names and faces on the unknown dead. Some of these heroes include my colleagues and friends: Dr. Steve Clark, database architect; Annette Davis, DNA analyst; Dr. Randy Hanzlick, medical examiner; Joanna Hughes, forensic artist; Todd Matthews, missing persons specialist; Chief Mark Whittaker, cold case investigator; Dr. Franklin Wright, forensic odontologist; anthropologist Dr. Bruce Anderson; and my many other dear and skillful associates in the field of forensic anthropology, who are too numerous to name. All of these individuals continue to move the science and art of human identification into the future.

Part of my own identity has found its way into the future in the form of my wonderful grandchildren, Naomi Jayne and Violet Elizabeth Bucher, to whom I dedicate this book.

Twenty-First Century Books
A division of Lerner Publishing Group, Inc.
241 First Avenue North
Minneapolis, MN 55401 U.S.A.

Website address: www.lernerbooks.com

Main body text set in Bell MT Std Semibold 12/15.
Typeface provided by Monotype Typography.

Library of Congress Cataloging-in-Publication Data

Murray, Elizabeth A.
    Forensic identification : putting a name and face on death / by Elizabeth A.
    Murray, PhD.
       p.   cm.
    Includes bibliographical references and index.
    ISBN 978-0-7613-6696-6 (lib. bdg. : alk. paper)
    1. Forensic sciences—Juvenile literature. I. Title.
HV8073.8.M877 2013
363.25—dc23   2011045218

Manufactured in the United States of America
1 – DP – 7/15/12

CONTENTS

THE UNIDENTIFIED DEAD

Every day, people whose identities are unknown are found dead. Some have been murdered, and some have been killed in accidents, natural disasters, genocides, wars, or terrorist attacks. In some cases, the cause and manner of death are not even known. Forensic investigators in the United States and Canada refer to any unidentified dead man—no matter how he died—as John Doe (in some other parts of the world, the name Joe Bloggs is used). An unknown deceased woman is known as Jane Doe in the United States and Canada, and an unidentified dead child may be referred to as Baby Doe. The investigators have the responsibility of figuring out who these people are and how they died.

Bodies that have been mutilated or that have been severely injured in terrible accidents can be extremely difficult to identify. For example, house fires, plane crashes, and the collapse of buildings can result in so much physical damage to human bodies that there's sometimes very little remaining of what once was a person. Natural disasters, such as earthquakes, floods, landslides, tsunamis, and hurricanes, may result in the loss of many lives over large geographic distances, dramatically slowing the process of identifying victims. The extreme forces of wind and water can carry bodies great distances and even strip people of personal items such as wallets and jewelry that would be

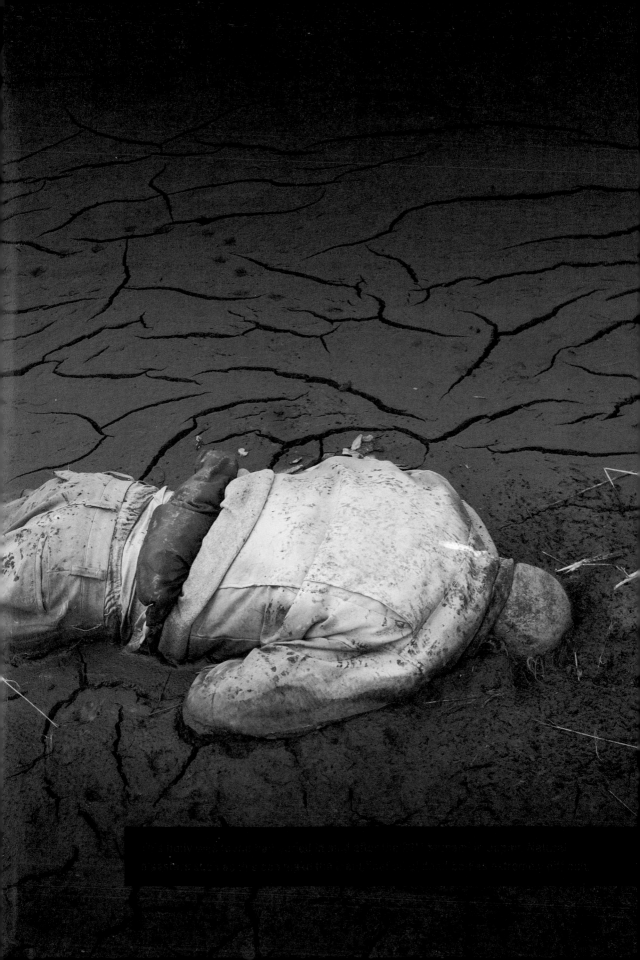

CASE FILE 1

A deer hunter and his dog walking in the woods come across skeletal remains. Some of the bones are scattered, but most lie in a pile beneath a tree. Some tattered clothes and the barrel of a handgun are visible beneath the leaves that cover the remains. Who was this person?

CASE FILE 2

While patrolling a nature preserve one cold morning, a park ranger discovers a human torso on a path leading deeper into the woods. The next day, a county sanitation worker is shocked when he sees two human legs poking from a torn garbage bag in a Dumpster. Later the same afternoon, in yet a third location, a man taking a winter walk discovers the severed head of a young woman along the side of the road. Are these body parts linked, and if so, who is this victim?

useful in identification. Many people may lose their lives in a single mass disaster, resulting in a confusing jumble of remains.

In the United States alone, about four thousand unidentified deceased persons are discovered every year. About three thousand are positively identified within the first year after their bodies are found. But the remaining one thousand unknown individuals are still nameless more than a year after being discovered. Some estimates suggest a total of as many as forty thousand unresolved John, Jane, and Baby Doe forensic cases currently exist in the United States.

GONE MISSING

As many as two-thirds of the open cases of unidentified persons in the United States involve badly decomposed or skeletonized remains. About one-fifth of the open U.S. cases of unidentified dead are those in which the body was discovered quickly enough that the person could have been able to be identified from facial features. Photographs of these people are often released to the media as part of the identification process. Yet some of these individuals are never positively identified. They may be estranged from their families and not reported missing, or they may live on the edges of society and may have no one to look out for them. In other cases, the distance or time between where or when a person disappears and where and when a body is found is so great that a connection is never made.

Some individuals purposely choose to disappear. They may be wanted by the law, owe large debts they cannot repay, or be in other kinds of trouble or danger from which they want to escape. Other people are missing because they have met with foul play such as kidnapping, murder, and other crimes. Whether missing by choice or by force, attempts may be made to hide a person's identity. For example, a living person can change his or her name and appearance. Or a murderer may mutilate a dead body to make the victim less easily identifiable.

Depending on environmental conditions, any deceased person may become harder to identify. After death, the natural processes of decay can quickly alter the visual appearance of a person, including facial features and skin color. The decomposition process results in the loss of fingerprints and ultimately all soft tissues such as skin and muscle. Eventually, decay usually leaves little but bones and teeth. Even a skeleton may completely return to the earth after a very long period of time. Under extreme conditions, such as exposure to acidic soil or incineration, this can happen more quickly. The rate of decomposition depends on many things, such as air or water temperature, exposure to animals (especially insects), soil chemistry, and other environmental factors.

The amount and type of body tissues remaining in deceased persons are a major factor in determining the methods that forensic scientists use for identification. A positive identification, however, does not require only some part of the human body. It also requires the ability to find features unique to that body and to then scientifically link those characteristics to what is known about a particular missing person. Only by matching specific, unusual, or unique traits of unknown persons to those of known individuals are reliable forensic identifications made.

IDENTIFIABLY UNIQUE

Human beings have a tremendous amount in common when you think about it. Normal growth and development result in standard physical features. We all have a head, arms, legs, and a torso. The body parts in all of us include bones, teeth, skin, muscles, and other organs. All body structures are made up of cells that unite to form patterns of tissues generally shared by all humans.

The genetic molecule known as deoxyribonucleic acid (DNA) is in the nucleus of all human body cells. DNA directs the growth and development of tissues, including the attributes that are common to all people.

And it is DNA that determines our variable features, such as hair color, eye color, skin color, height, blood type, and other characteristics.

In addition to the genetic information that determines who we are, our outside environment also influences body structures and functions. People's health, nutrition, personal choices, and where they live all impact their physical makeup. For example, if children do not have exercise and a good diet, they will probably not reach the full height that their genetics would allow. Basic body structure is permanently changed when a person has a badly healed broken arm, an implanted artificial knee, or a dental filling. Choices such as smoking and drug use or unintentional exposure to harmful substances in the environment can make one person's body different from another. Tattoos, scars, and the way skin is affected by old age and sun exposure also add variation to an individual's appearance. Every person's physical uniqueness comes partly from genetics and partly from environment and lifestyle.

Other things that contribute to differences in outward appearances include the way people dress. Individuals also make choices about what they carry in their purse or wallet. But personal effects, such as cell phones, clothing, jewelry, or a driver's license, are not considered forms of positive identification. Positive identification comes from some part of the body that can

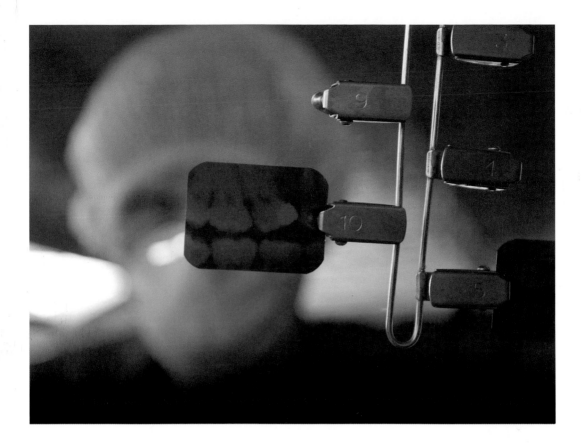

be scientifically confirmed as belonging to a specific person. This may include facial features, birthmarks, or DNA. Positive identification is also often made from parts that were not "original equipment," such as dental fillings, surgical implants, and tattoos.

Many different types of forensic scientists and experts may be involved in identifying a body. Fingerprint specialists take prints from unidentified persons for comparison to existing fingerprint records. Medical doctors trained as forensic pathologists perform autopsies on unidentified bodies in search of any features or tissues that may be helpful in establishing identity. Specialized dentists, known as forensic odontologists, carefully chart the teeth of the unknown dead for potential comparison to records of missing persons. DNA experts use body tissue samples to create genetic profiles of John and Jane Does for comparison to other DNA profiles. If the remains are only bones, forensic anthropologists and facial reconstruction artists offer scientific insight into how a person may have looked when alive. Law enforcement officers investigate leads and gather records from missing persons for comparisons.

IDENTIFICATION MATTERS

Positive identification of a dead body allows authorities to create an official death certificate. This document provides the name of the dead person along with the date and cause and manner of death, if known. In some cases—such as the collapse of the World Trade Center buildings in the terrorist attacks of September 11, 2001, or Hurricane Katrina, which hit New Orleans in 2005—missing persons are sometimes declared dead even though their bodies are not recovered. This requires a waiting period followed by a special court order.

Proof of death is vital for many reasons. Psychologists have shown that it is difficult for people to grieve a dead loved one until and unless they know for certain that a person they care for is actually deceased. Even though someone may be gone for many years and assumed to be dead, that person's loved ones often hold out hope until they know for sure the missing person will never return. Even those who have given up hope still live with unanswered questions. Learning that a loved one is truly dead and gone forever provides an important sense of resolution, even though the confirmation of the loss can be tragic news.

Positive identification is also a practical matter. For example, once the identity of a murder victim is known, law enforcement officers may have a better chance of locating the person responsible for the death. This is especially true in cases where the deceased person and the killer knew each other. In those instances, establishing who the victim was may lead directly to a suspect. Further, if the criminal is unknown but left physical evidence of his or her own identity at a crime scene, personal identification methods can be used to find the offender. For example, if the criminal left behind fingerprints, body fluids, or DNA, similar forensic tests used on unknown deceased persons can be applied to help identify a living suspect.

Positive identification also means that life insurance money and other forms of inheritance can be released to survivors. Certifying the death of a spouse permits a widow to legally remarry. Proof of death of a child's parents allows for legal plans to be put in place for the care of that orphaned child.

COUNTY OF LOS ANGELES • REGISTRAR–RECORDER/COUNTY CLERK

3052012025719

CERTIFICATE OF DEATH
STATE OF CALIFORNIA
USE BLACK INK ONLY / NO ERASURES, WHITEOUTS OR ALTERATIONS
VS-11 (REV 3/06)

STATE FILE NUMBER

3201219005767

LOCAL REGISTRATION NUMBER

DECEDENT'S PERSONAL DATA

1. NAME OF DECEDENT—FIRST (Given)	2. MIDDLE	3. LAST (Family)
WHITNEY	ELIZABETH	HOUSTON

AKA, ALSO KNOWN AS – Include full AKA (FIRST, MIDDLE, LAST)

4. DATE OF BIRTH mm/dd/ccyy	5. AGE Yrs.	IF UNDER ONE YEAR — Months / Days	IF UNDER 24 HOURS — Hours / Minutes	6. SEX
08/09/1963	48			F

9. BIRTH STATE/FOREIGN COUNTRY	10. SOCIAL SECURITY NUMBER	11. EVER IN U.S. ARMED FORCES?	12. MARITAL STATUS/SRDP (at Time of Death)	7. DATE OF DEATH mm/dd/ccyy	8. HOUR (24 Hours)
NEW JERSEY		YES [X] NO [ ] UNK	DIVORCED	02/11/2012	1555

13. EDUCATION – Highest Level/Degree	14/15. WAS DECEDENT HISPANIC/LATINO(A)/SPANISH?	16. DECEDENT'S RACE – Up to 3 races may be listed (see worksheet on back)
ASSOCIATE	[ ] YES [X] NO	AFRICAN AMERICAN

17. USUAL OCCUPATION – Type of work for most of life. DO NOT USE RETIRED	18. KIND OF BUSINESS OR INDUSTRY (e.g., grocery store, road construction, employment agency, etc.)	19. YEARS IN OCCUPATION
ENTERTAINER	ENTERTAINMENT	33

USUAL RESIDENCE

20. DECEDENT'S RESIDENCE (Street and number, or location)
9046 RIVER MANOR

21. CITY	22. COUNTY/PROVINCE	23. ZIP CODE	24. YEARS IN COUNTY	25. STATE/FOREIGN COUNTRY
ALPHARETTA	FULTON	30022	48	GEORGIA

INFORMANT

26. INFORMANT'S NAME, RELATIONSHIP	27. INFORMANT'S MAILING ADDRESS (Street and number, or rural route number, city or town, state and zip)
BOBBI KRISTINA BROWN, DAUGHTER	9046 RIVER MANOR, ALPHARETTA, GA 30022

SPOUSE/SRDP AND PARENT INFORMATION

28. NAME OF SURVIVING SPOUSE/SRDP—FIRST	29. MIDDLE	30. LAST (BIRTH NAME)
-	-	-

31. NAME OF FATHER/PARENT—FIRST	32. MIDDLE	33. LAST	34. BIRTH STATE
JOHN	RUSSELL	HOUSTON	NEW JERSEY

35. NAME OF MOTHER/PARENT—FIRST	36. MIDDLE	37. LAST BIRTH NAME	38. BIRTH STATE
EMILY	CISSY	DRINKARD	NEW JERSEY

FUNERAL DIRECTOR/LOCAL REGISTRAR

39. DISPOSITION DATE mm/dd/ccyy	40. PLACE OF FINAL DISPOSITION
02/18/2012	FAIR VIEW CEMETERY 1100 EAST BROAD STREET WESTFIELD, NJ 07090

41. TYPE OF DISPOSITION(S)	43. LICENSE NUMBER
TR/BU	EMB8087

44. NAME OF FUNERAL ESTABLISHMENT	46. SIGNATURE OF LOCAL REGISTRAR
HOUSE OF WINSTON MORTUARY INC. FD639	02/13/2012

PLACE OF DEATH

101. PLACE OF DEATH	102. IF HOSPITAL SPECIFY ONE	103. IF OTHER THAN HOSPITAL SPECIFY ONE
BEVERLY HILTON HOTEL	IP/OP [ ] ER/OP [ ] DOA [ ]	[ ] ... [X] Other

104. COUNTY	105. FACILITY ADDRESS OR LOCATION WHERE FOUND (Street and number, or location)	CITY
LOS ANGELES	9876 WILSHIRE BOULEVARD	BEVERLY HILLS

CAUSE OF DEATH

107. CAUSE OF DEATH Enter the chain of events — diseases, injuries, or complications — that directly caused the death. DO NOT enter terminal events such as cardiac arrest, respiratory arrest, or ventricular fibrillation without showing the etiology.

		Time Interval Between Onset and Death	108. DEATH REPORTED TO CORONER?
IMMEDIATE CAUSE (Final disease or condition resulting in death)	(A) DEFERRED		[X] YES [ ] NO
	(AT)	-	REFERRAL NUMBER 2012-01022
Sequentially list conditions, if any, leading to cause on Line A. Enter UNDERLYING CAUSE (disease or injury that initiated the events resulting in death) LAST	(BT)		109. BIOPSY PERFORMED? [ ] YES [X] NO
	(CT)		110. AUTOPSY PERFORMED? [X] YES [ ] NO
	(DT)		111. USED IN DETERMINING CAUSE? [X] YES [ ] NO

112. OTHER SIGNIFICANT CONDITIONS CONTRIBUTING TO DEATH BUT NOT RESULTING IN THE UNDERLYING CAUSE GIVEN IN 107
NONE

113. WAS OPERATION PERFORMED FOR ANY CONDITION (ITEM 107 OR 112? (If yes, list type of operation and date.)
NO

113A. IF FEMALE, PREGNANT IN LAST YEAR?
[ ] YES [X] NO [ ] UNK

PHYSICIAN'S CERTIFICATION

114. I CERTIFY THAT TO THE BEST OF MY KNOWLEDGE DEATH OCCURRED AT THE HOUR, DATE, AND PLACE STATED FROM THE CAUSES STATED.	115. SIGNATURE AND TITLE OF CERTIFIER	116. LICENSE NUMBER	117. DATE mm/dd/ccyy
Decedent Attended Since / Decedent Last Seen Alive			

118. TYPE ATTENDING PHYSICIAN'S NAME, MAILING ADDRESS, ZIP CODE

CORONER'S USE ONLY

119. I CERTIFY THAT IN MY OPINION DEATH OCCURRED AT THE HOUR, DATE, AND PLACE STATED FROM THE CAUSES STATED.	120. INJURED AT WORK?	121. INJURY DATE mm/dd/ccyy	122. HOUR (24 Hours)
MANNER OF DEATH: [ ] Natural [ ] Accident [ ] Homicide [ ] Suicide [X] Pending Investigation [ ] Could not be determined	[ ] YES [ ] NO [ ] UNK		

123. PLACE OF INJURY (e.g., home, construction site, wooded area, etc.)

124. DESCRIBE HOW INJURY OCCURRED (Events which resulted in injury)

125. LOCATION OF INJURY (Street and number, or location, and city and zip)

126. SIGNATURE OF CORONER / DEPUTY CORONER	127. DATE mm/dd/ccyy	128. TYPE NAME, TITLE OF CORONER / DEPUTY CORONER
	02/13/2012	REGINA M AUGUSTINE, DEPUTY CORONER

STATE REGISTRAR

A	B	C	D	E	FAX AUTH.#	CENSUS TRACT

010001001990560

This is to certify that this document is a true copy of the official record filed with the Registrar-Recorder/County Clerk.

FEB 16 2012

001526359

Dean C. Logan
DEAN C. LOGAN
Registrar-Recorder/County Clerk

This copy not valid unless prepared on engraved border displaying the Seal and Signature of the Registrar-Recorder/County Clerk.
PRNO3 (82V) 07/11

ANY ALTERATION OR ERASURE VOIDS THIS CERTIFICATE

CLOSING THE CASE

When a deer hunter found a pile of bones beneath a tree in the woods, police were called to the scene. One of the officers knew that one year earlier, an abandoned car had been found on a nearby road. The car belonged to a middle-aged man who had gone missing at the same time his abandoned car was found. The officer had been investigating the man's disappearance, but the man had never been located.

When the police discovered the car, they had questioned the man's family. They learned that the missing man had been diagnosed with cancer just prior to his disappearance. Family members told police that the man was extremely upset and depressed by the diagnosis, that he had been out of work for a year, and that he had no health insurance. His wife also reported that one of his handguns was missing from the gun safe at their home after he vanished. His family feared the worst.

Those facts alone were not enough to prove that the human skeleton discovered a year later was the missing man. Scientific links were needed to establish positive identification. First, a forensic anthropologist examined the bones and confirmed that they were most likely those of a middle-aged man. A forensic pathologist then determined that the man's skull showed a close contact gunshot wound to the head. Police investigators had recovered a handgun at the scene and found that it was legally registered to the missing man. A forensic scientist showed that the single bullet found among the bones had come from that gun. Finally, a DNA sample taken from the skeleton was compared to the DNA profile of the man's sister. The two DNA samples showed the same pattern, and a positive identification was made. Based on the circumstantial (indirect) evidence and the statements given by the family, the coroner ruled this man's death a suicide.

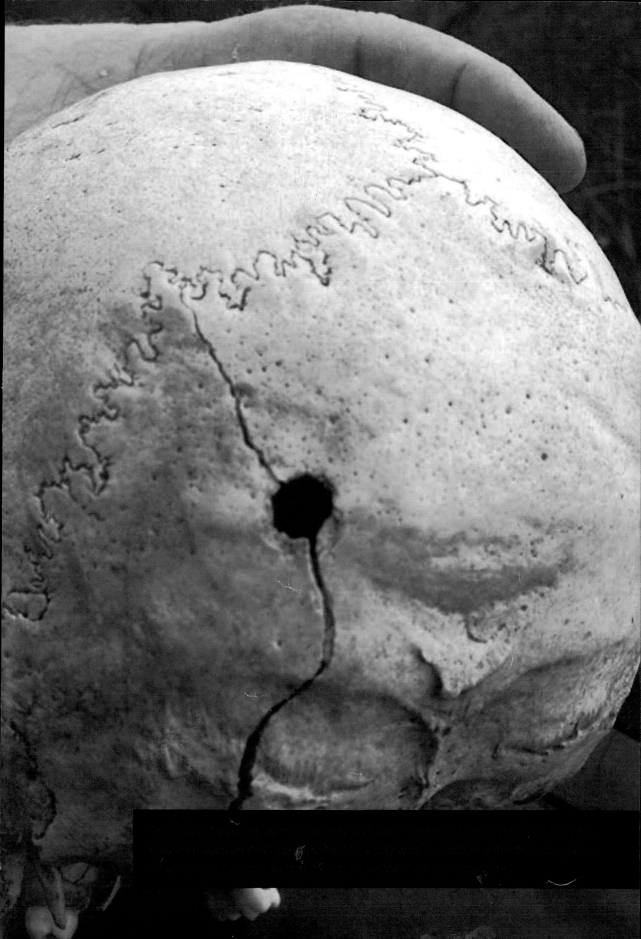

CASE FILE 2

When isolated body parts turned up in several locations over a two-day period, investigators first needed to determine whether they were searching for the identity of one person or multiple individuals. Because the discovery occurred in winter, cold temperatures had preserved the remains. This gave the investigation a big advantage. Even though the body had been dismembered, its surface features were largely intact.

On the first day remains were found, when most of a human torso was recovered, the medical examiner could tell that the body was that of an adult Caucasian female. The pathologist determined that the extreme loss of blood from the dismemberment probably made the skin of the corpse look much paler than the woman had appeared when she was alive. Her skin had an average amount of body fat in its deepest layer. From these findings, the medical examiner could assume only that the torso belonged to an adult, white female of average weight.

The next morning, crime scene investigators brought the medical examiner portions of two human legs that had been found in a garbage Dumpster. Each of the legs had been cut just below the knee. However, they could not be directly associated to the torso even though the legs had pale skin, identical to the color of the remains already in the morgue. In addition, the legs had been shaved hairless and the toenails were painted. These practices are typically only seen in some adult women. The medical examiner believed that the body parts probably reflected a single terrible crime.

Later that same afternoon, the horrific roadside discovery of a young woman's head turned out to be the key in this investigation. The winter temperatures had perfectly preserved her facial features. Furthermore, the severed skin on the woman's neck matched the cut edges of the skin on the torso found the previous day and confirmed a link between these cases.

The medical examiner believed that anyone who knew this person would recognize her by sight. A decision was made to take a picture of the woman's face and release it to the media. A sheet was pulled

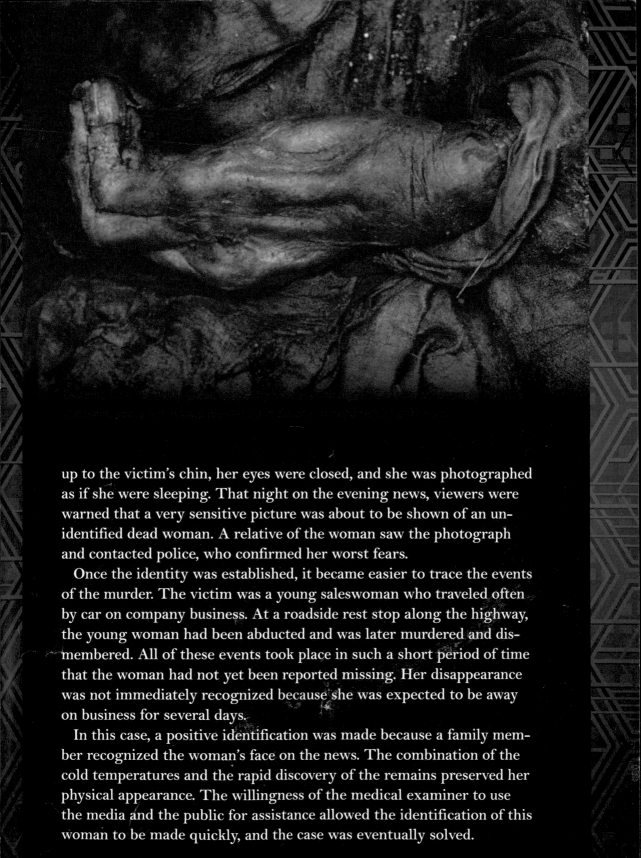

up to the victim's chin, her eyes were closed, and she was photographed as if she were sleeping. That night on the evening news, viewers were warned that a very sensitive picture was about to be shown of an unidentified dead woman. A relative of the woman saw the photograph and contacted police, who confirmed her worst fears.

Once the identity was established, it became easier to trace the events of the murder. The victim was a young saleswoman who traveled often by car on company business. At a roadside rest stop along the highway, the young woman had been abducted and was later murdered and dismembered. All of these events took place in such a short period of time that the woman had not yet been reported missing. Her disappearance was not immediately recognized because she was expected to be away on business for several days.

In this case, a positive identification was made because a family member recognized the woman's face on the news. The combination of the cold temperatures and the rapid discovery of the remains preserved her physical appearance. The willingness of the medical examiner to use the media and the public for assistance allowed the identification of this woman to be made quickly, and the case was eventually solved.

SKIN DEEP

STAYING ON THE SURFACE

The surface of the human body is covered with its largest and most familiar organ—the skin. Openings in the skin make way for common features such as eyes and a mouth. The skin drapes over structures that create the familiar framework of the body. These underlying components include bones, muscles, ligaments, tendons, and the cartilages of the nose and ears. All the structures of the body come together in typical patterns that are commonly shared among humans.

The body's surface, however, is not completely generic. Human skin, hair, and eyes come in a variety of colors, and external features exhibit different shapes and sizes. Our outward appearances also change with time. Hairs and nails, embedded in the skin, are constantly replenished. They grow and change over a person's life, as does the skin itself. Scars and tattoos also contribute to the way a person looks. We rely on our eyes and brain to sort out the fairly minor external differences among people, so we can tell those we know from those we don't.

In terms of forensic identification, nothing specific about death immediately changes a dead person's outward appearance. Unless an accident or other trauma has disfigured the body, a person who has just died may look the same as when sleeping. Therefore, in the early stages of a forensic investigation, the skin is key to providing clues that forensic scientists use when trying to identify the remains of an unknown person.

CASE FILE 3

One summer evening, two boys fishing along a small river notice a foul odor coming from the bushes near where they are sitting. When they investigate, they find that the smell is coming from a decomposing human body that is hung up on the bank of the river. The bloated corpse is intact and face up on the water's edge. However, the face is so distorted and puffy that what the boys see is hardly recognizable as a human face. Skin discoloration from decay makes it hard to determine the dead man's ethnicity. What external features, if any, can be used for identification in a case like this?

CASE FILE 4

Early one morning, construction workers begin arriving on their job site in the downtown area of a large city. In the corner of the lot where they park their vehicles, one of the workers discovers the body of a man who appears to be dead. The body is lying in a pool of blood, and it looks as if the man has been badly beaten and stabbed in the chest. There are no signs of decomposition, but the injuries to the dead man's face are so severe that his features cannot be identified. He is wearing a sleeveless T-shirt, jeans, and sneakers and has pale skin and straight, black hair. The witnesses notice several tattoos on his shoulders and arms. A glint of metal near his bloody left eye could be from a pierced eyebrow. His shirt is pulled up, revealing a scar on his lower abdomen. Can all these details provide identification for a man whose face is so badly injured?

Soon after death, however, the process of decay begins. On the other hand, if the surrounding temperature is extremely low, a body will be preserved indefinitely. As a body decomposes and chemical changes progress, external features rapidly change. Skin color is altered, and bacteria within the body produce gases that bloat the corpse. Other living creatures may begin to feed on body tissues. These creatures include certain types of insects that lay their eggs in body openings. Once the process of decay is advanced, a dead body can be unrecognizable, even to close friends or family members.

BODY SURFACE BASICS

Human skin has three main layers: the epidermis, the dermis, and the subcutaneous layer. Depending on its location on the body, skin bears hair, glands, and nails. The epidermis is the outermost part of the skin. It is filled with many layers of tightly packed cells filled with a waterproof protein known as keratin. The epidermis helps form a protective barrier to the outside world. The surface layer of the epidermis consists of dead cells that are routinely shed.

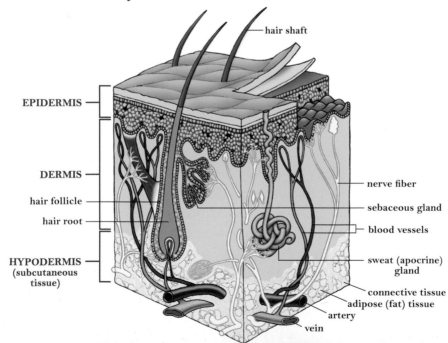

This diagram shows the three main levels of skin: the epidermis, the dermis, and the subcutaneous. It also shows hair, glands, blood vessels, and other features of human skin.

Beneath the epidermis is the dermis. The dermis is rich with blood vessels that carry nutrients to all skin cells, including those deep in the epidermis. The dermis is also loaded with protein fibers, some made of the strong protein collagen and others made of a more elastic protein. These give the skin strength and flexibility. Beneath the dermis is subcutaneous fat. The thickness of this fatty layer varies in different parts of the body and changes when a person gains or loses weight.

When the skin is injured, damage to the epidermis usually heals well, because its cells are good at reproducing themselves. An injury that extends to the dermis, however, often leaves permanent marks. A deep wound opens blood vessels, can destroy hair follicles, and may harm other internal skin structures. When the dermis heals, new protein fibers form, although they are not laid down in the same pattern as the original ones. The result is a visible change to the skin's exterior that we call a scar. When skin is expanded beyond the limits of the elastic proteins in the dermis, another type of scar called a stretch mark may result. Old age limits the body's ability to replenish the supportive collagen protein in the dermis, so the skin wrinkles over time. The traces left by injuries and old age are only some of the ways human skin differs from one person to another.

SKIN COLOR

Genetic variations among people around the world result in a wide range of skin colors. Healthy skin tones range from pale pink to the deepest shades of brown. Skin color is inherited, and skin color can vary widely, even within one family. Skin tones are somewhat associated with ancestry. This is due to slight genetic differences among people whose heritage began in diverse parts of the world.

Two main protein pigments create skin color. A red protein called hemoglobin is packed within the body's red blood cells and gives blood its color. How much hemoglobin can be seen in the vessels of the dermis when looking at the skin's surface is determined by the amount of the pigment melanin in the epidermis of the skin. Melanin comes in two main varieties—a yellow-to-red form and a brown-to-black form. People whose epidermis makes a lot of dark melanin will have very deeply colored skin through which not much hemoglobin can be seen. Their skin will be brown. People who produce very little melanin in their skin will have a nearly transparent epidermis. They will have a pink tone to their skin.

This is due to the red hemoglobin in the dermis, as seen through the pale epidermis. Variations in the types of melanin people produce result in skin tones that appear more yellow, somewhat reddish, or olive brown.

PIGMENT PATCHES

Freckles, moles, and birthmarks contribute to making one person's skin more unique than another's. These surface spots come from areas of the skin that produce excess pigment. Birthmarks are usually present when a baby is born and tend to occur randomly. Freckles can develop after sun exposure, and the tendency to be freckled is inherited. Moles are usually raised patches of skin that contain lots of melanin-producing cells, though the color of moles can vary.

Many people develop moles and other pigmented patches on their skin as they age, especially as environmental damage to skin accumulates. On the other hand, freckles may naturally fade over time, and it is possible to remove most of these other surface features through various medical treatments.

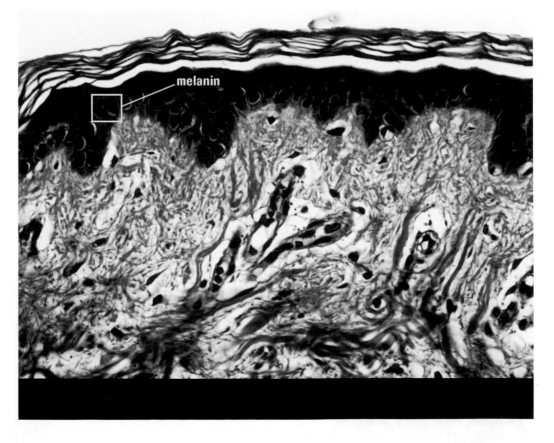
melanin

EYES AND HAIR

Eye color is another pigment-related external feature that distinguishes some people from others. The type and amount of melanin produced in the part of the eye known as the iris is largely responsible for the color of a person's eyes. As with skin color, eye color is inherited.

Melanin also determines the color of a person's hair. Since melanin comes in yellow-to-red and brown-to-black varieties, the amount and type of melanin in the root of a growing hair establishes the hair shaft's natural color. In old age, protein production slows down in the body and a person may make less melanin in the scalp. Hair will then lose its color and become white. Some individuals totally stop producing hair shafts as they age and become bald. Genetic differences among people help determine not only hair color and the tendency to lose hair but also the general form and texture of hair.

IDENTIFYING THE EXTERNALS

When an intact human body is discovered soon after death, the person is often recognizable. In instances where there is a presumed identity, the victim's family members or close friends may be asked to view the body and make an identification. If authorities have no suspected identity and facial features are still obvious, investigators can photograph the deceased and release an image to the media. Anyone who recognizes the face can call in with information to help identify the dead person.

A thorough external examination of a dead body is always performed at autopsy. One purpose of this exam is to record all surface features that may aid in establishing identity, if the person is unknown. Scars or stretch marks provide clues about a person's medical history and life story. A scar can indicate a prior surgery or a serious accident at some time in the past. Stretch marks on the abdomen of a Jane Doe may suggest a previous pregnancy. Wrinkles may indicate the body is that of an older person.

Tattoos, piercings, and other body art are also unique signs of a person's identity. Because tattoo ink is injected deep into the dermis, a tattoo is permanent. A name or date in a tattoo can be an extremely valuable clue in an investigation. Forensic scientists who are familiar with styles of body art can use their knowledge to aid in identification of a dead person. A tattoo may also show that a person belonged to a specific group. For example, certain images and symbols represent gang membership, sexual orientation, prison history, or military affiliation.

This photograph shows a strand of human hair. Forensic investigators can tell a lot about the color and other characteristics of the hair of a dead person from microscopic examination.

Using external features to identify a John or Jane Doe, however, is complicated by decomposition. Unless a corpse is found and preserved quickly, changes in body chemistry will drastically alter a person's appearance. As decay proceeds, the color of skin and eyes changes. Blood seeps from vessels into nearby tissues and alters their natural color. Light-colored skin can darken as blood pools in tissues, and dark skin can lighten as the epidermis decays. Eyes become cloudy, making the color of pigments in the iris difficult and ultimately impossible to judge. Body cells begin to break down and spill out their contents, altering the composition of tissues. This can make facial features unrecognizable. In time, tattoos, scars, stretch marks, and wrinkles are no longer visible. In addition, bacteria and other organisms can feed off decaying tissues and affect the appearance of both external and deeper body features.

Hair color, form, and texture do not change significantly during decomposition. Because hair shafts are already made up of dead tissue, any color or texture changes a person made to hair during life will remain after death. Investigators know that chemical treatments on hair can straighten curls or add curl to hair that was naturally straight. So they can examine hair under a microscope to tell whether or not the color or texture is natural or artificial, since this may help with the identification process.

TOUCHING A BIT OF HISTORY

Fingerprints have been used for centuries in identification. Evidence suggests that the Chinese may have used fingerprints as a sign of identity perhaps as long ago as three thousand years. Historical accounts from a variety of cultures across time show that fingerprints were used to designate the artist of a painting or piece of pottery. In Europe the scientific study of fingerprints dates back to at least the 1600s, when researchers began to draw and classify the specific patterns observed on the skin of human hands. In the mid-1800s in India, the British adopted the local custom of using fingerprints as signatures on documents to identify people within the Indian territories ruled by Britain. In the United States, fingerprints came into common forensic use in the early 1900s, beginning first in the state of New York and quickly spreading to the rest of the country.

FINGERPRINTS

While the range of skin, hair, and eye colors is limited among humans, prints from human fingers, palms, and soles of feet are completely unique to each person. For this reason, forensic scientists use prints for a variety of identification purposes. People who want to evade the law have tried to alter their fingerprint patterns. Severe burns from either heat or chemicals can destroy fingerprints, but the scars that result end up being as unique and identifiable as the original print patterns.

Genetics determine that humans will develop fingerprints. However, the intricate designs those prints take do not come only from heredity. No two people share the same fingerprint patterns, not even identical twins. Since identical twins possess the exact same DNA, developmental factors must also aid in creating a person's fingerprints. Although prints enlarge as hands grow, the general pattern of a fingerprint never changes.

Fingerprints are unique to each individual human being. These prints come from three different people. Patterns like these help investigators establish identity.

Skin of the palms and soles is different from skin elsewhere on the body because it does not have hair or oil glands. It also has an extra thick and tough layer in the epidermis. The surface ridges on the palms of hands and the soles of feet are created by tiny raised areas in the dermis, which are called dermal papillae. As the thick epidermis folds over the top of the dermal papillae, fingerprints, palm prints, and ridge patterns on the soles of the feet result. Even though the body constantly sheds the surface of the epidermis, prints from fingers, palms, and the soles of feet are not lost because their pattern is rooted in the more stable dermis.

WHORLS, ARCHES, AND LOOPS

Scientists have several ways to classify fingerprints. The three major patterns are known as whorls, arches, and loops. Additional smaller characteristics within each pattern, known as minutiae, include tiny features that add to the uniqueness of a print. Some of these minutiae are ridges that are so small that they form only a dot or a little island. Other minor features include ridges that split like a fork or come to an abrupt ending. Even the microscopic patterns of sweat gland openings contribute to the individuality of a single print.

When the body of an unknown person is discovered and decomposition is not too advanced, investigators can take fingerprints from the body. This involves inking and printing the skin of the deceased. Any skin or skin fragment from recovered fingers, palms, or the soles of the feet may yield prints. Sometimes during the early stages of decay, the epidermis may peel away from the dermis. Investigators can even use pieces of shed epidermis from the hands to obtain fingerprints or partial prints. If a body is severely decomposed or badly burned, however, the epidermis is unsuitable for fingerprinting.

YOUR PRINTS OR MINE?

Print comparisons have solved countless crimes and identified many unknown bodies. But for fingerprints to be useful in establishing positive identification, a John or Jane Doe has to have known fingerprint samples stored somewhere. People who routinely have fingerprint records on file include bank tellers, teachers, military personnel, and those who have been arrested, among others. These records are kept for a variety of reasons such as bank security, child safety, identification of criminals, and identifying the dead.

In the past, investigators had to search stored files of inked finger-print cards by hand to make comparisons. This often meant they had to already have a good idea of who the unknown person was to better lead them to likely comparisons. Over time, fingerprint experts developed coding systems as a form of shorthand that would summarize the patterns on each finger. This allowed for more rapid decisions regarding whose prints might make a good comparison.

In the late twentieth century, computerized systems were developed to search and compare print records. The fingerprints of an unknown person can be scanned into a computer and then compared across the Internet. In the United States, the Federal Bureau of Investigation (FBI) manages a system known as the Integrated Automated Fingerprint Identification System (IAFIS). Using this system, fingerprints of a John Doe found in one city can be compared against all the fingerprints in the country that are in the FBI's database. This can result in a positive identification even in investigations that began with authorities having no idea of the person's identity.

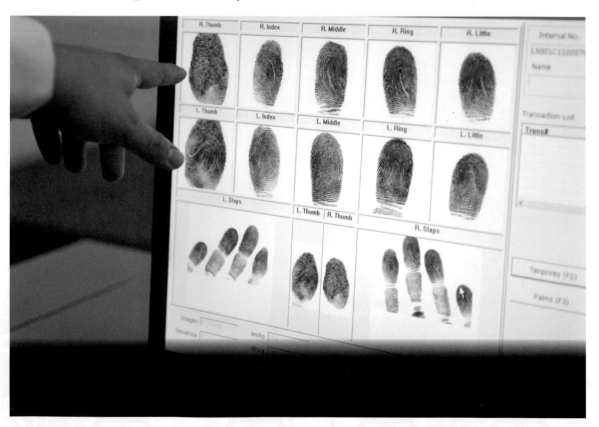

CLOSING THE CASE

When two boys discovered a decaying dead body along a river-bank, the police came to search the scene and remove the victim. They carefully transferred the remains to a body bag and took the waterlogged corpse to the coroner's office for an autopsy.

The coroner observed that the early stages of decomposition were well under way. Normal bacteria within the man's digestive system were producing gases, so the man's abdomen was badly bloated. Insects had begun to settle into the openings in his body and feed, leaving some facial features unrecognizable. In addition, decomposition changes had affected the man's skin tone, resulting in multicolored patches of discoloration. It was difficult to figure out the man's natural skin color. The man looked as though he probably had very little hair during life. His scalp was mostly bald, and what little head and facial hair he had was shaved close. The examination revealed no obvious visual clues from simply looking at this body, except to say the victim was male. The autopsy also revealed that the man had been shot in the chest, but the bullet had gone straight through the body and was not found.

A forensic investigator from the morgue had an idea that could possibly lead to identification. Even though some of the man's epidermis was separating from his body, it was still possible that any remaining pieces of skin from his hands would bear fingerprints. A careful inspection of the corpse revealed fingerprint ridges on the last three fingers of the left hand, which had been balled into a fist, possibly preserving the skin. A fingerprint recovery specialist carefully manipulated the victim's left hand and took prints. Even with only a partial set of fingerprints, the FBI fingerprint database (IAFIS) quickly got a hit.

The dead man turned out to be a drug dealer who had been in prison several times throughout his adult life. He was heavily involved in gang activity and had been living a difficult and violent life for several years. Based on their investigation, police heard that several local groups were fighting to increase their illegal drug sales in the area. The word on the street was that rival gang members shot the man and dumped his body in the river. Although the case was not immediately solved, the victim was positively identified through his fingerprint records. The man's body was released for burial to a grieving father who had been trying to help his troubled son turn his life around.

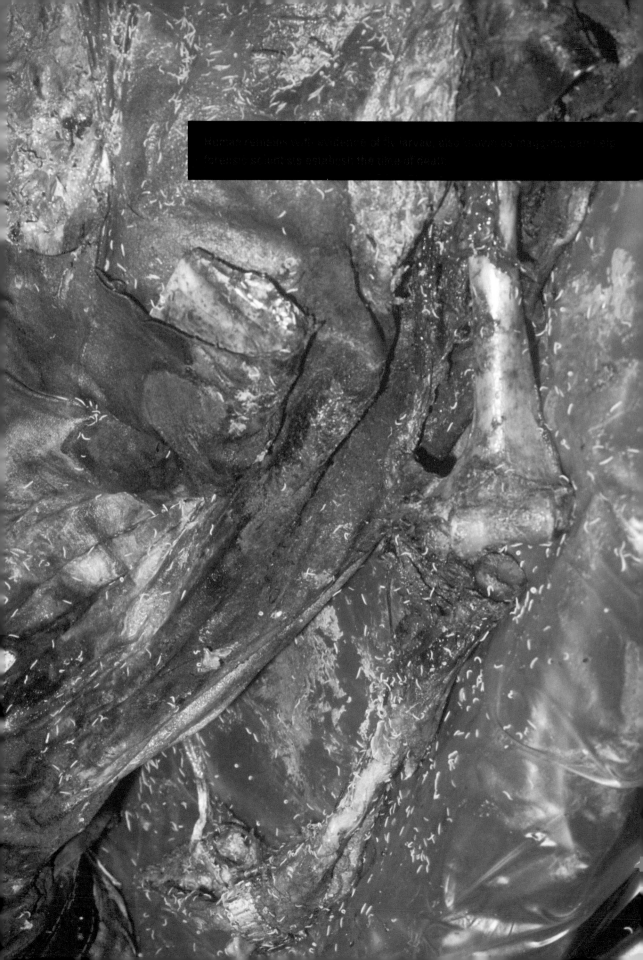

Human remains with evidence of fly larvae, also known as maggots, can help a forensic scientist establish the time of death.

Police were called to a construction site after workers found the body of a young man who had been murdered in the parking lot. The body was clothed, but officers found no wallet and no form of identification on the victim. The man's face had been so badly beaten that he was not recognizable. His sleeveless shirt showed evidence of a cut in the chest area and an apparent stab wound in the skin beneath. A pool of blood had collected around the man's head and torso.

Even at the scene, officers noted that the man's skin tone and straight dark hair suggested he might be of Asian descent. The man had a dragon tattoo on his right shoulder. Both of the man's arms had multiple tattoos, one of which appeared to represent Japanese or Chinese writing. A metal ring pierced the skin at the outer edge of his left eyebrow. The man wore his jeans low on his hips, and the bottom of his shirt was pulled up, revealing what appeared to be an old surgical scar on the right side of his lower abdomen.

Around the same time the body was being examined, a woman across town walked into a police station. She told officers that her son had gone out to a club the night before with his friends. When he did not come home, she became very concerned. Although her son had not been gone long enough for police to file an official missing persons report, they took information from her about her son. The woman said that he was an eighteen-year-old Asian American with short, straight, dark hair. She provided police with his height and weight. When asked about any other distinguishing features, the woman said her son had a pierced eyebrow, a dragon tattoo on his shoulder, and tattoos on both arms. In addition, her son had a scar on his belly where his appendix had been removed surgically when he was ten years old. She added that her son always wore a gold necklace that had been given to him by his father, who was now deceased.

Within moments after the woman left the police station, the officers who had taken her report learned of the body that had been discovered across town. The officers knew their missing man was very likely the homicide victim from the other side of town. They drove to the mother's address with the sad news that they feared her son was the victim of violence.

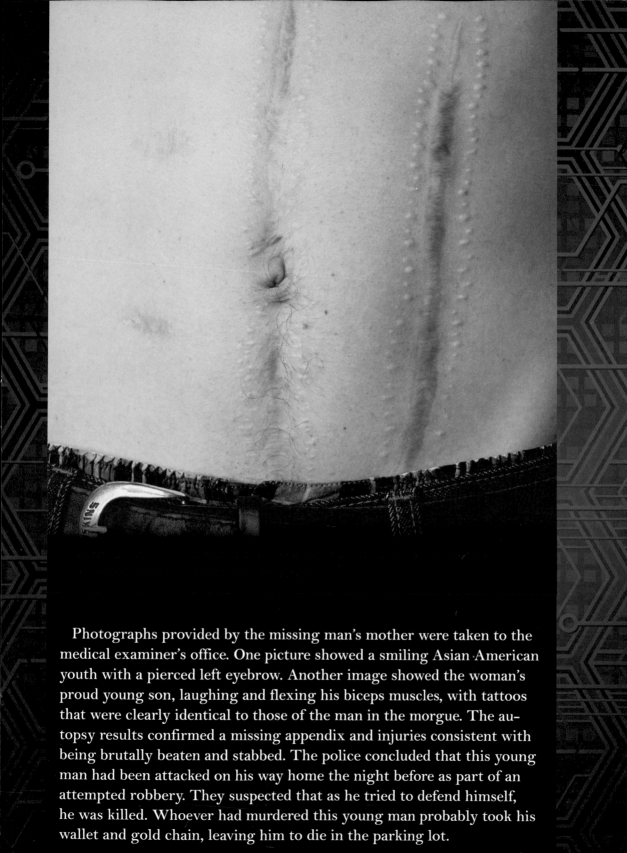

Photographs provided by the missing man's mother were taken to the medical examiner's office. One picture showed a smiling Asian American youth with a pierced left eyebrow. Another image showed the woman's proud young son, laughing and flexing his biceps muscles, with tattoos that were clearly identical to those of the man in the morgue. The autopsy results confirmed a missing appendix and injuries consistent with being brutally beaten and stabbed. The police concluded that this young man had been attacked on his way home the night before as part of an attempted robbery. They suspected that as he tried to defend himself, he was killed. Whoever had murdered this young man probably took his wallet and gold chain, leaving him to die in the parking lot.

chapter three

HARD PARTS

BONE BIOLOGY

The human skeletal system creates a framework for the soft tissues of the body. The size of a person's skeleton determines height, and dimensions of certain bones contribute to a body's overall build. These durable parts have important functions. For example, bones protect soft organs such as the brain, the heart, and lungs. The bones of the skeleton also produce blood cells for the body and serve as a warehouse for essential minerals. Muscles are attached to skeletal elements to allow movement at joints. Teeth are firmly rooted in the upper and lower jawbones to allow efficient chewing.

The basic structure of bony tissue consists of living bone cells surrounded by proteins and minerals. The protein collagen helps give bones enough flexibility to withstand impact without fracturing during normal activities. The mineral portion of bones makes them extremely strong. In fact, the materials that make up bones and teeth are the hardest natural substances in the body. For this reason, bones and teeth may remain long after decomposition degrades skin, muscles, and other organs.

FEELING IT IN THE BONES

During the earliest years of bone formation, some parts of the skeleton are made entirely of cartilage. Over time, this cartilage turns to bone

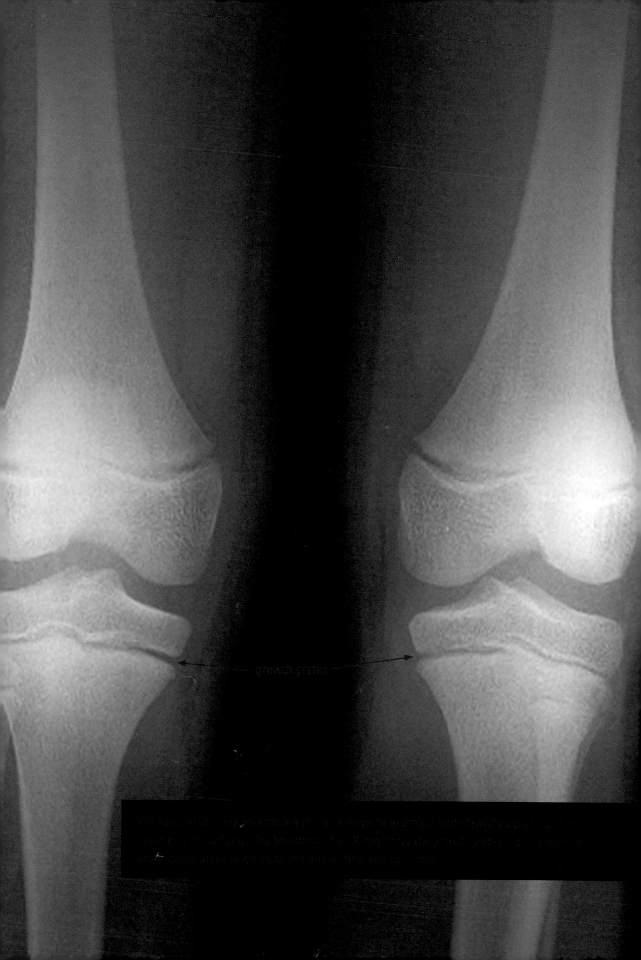

growth plates

CASE FILE 5

Several members of a power company crew pull their truck onto the shoulder of an old country road. They need to put in electric lines for new housing in the area. While clearing brush along the side of the road, one of the workers finds a rolled-up tarp. It looks as though the plastic sheeting is wrapped around a tattered bedspread. When the worker tries to move the bundle, a few bones and a small, decaying tennis shoe spill out of one end of the package. Are these human bones? If so, who was dumped here along the side of the road and when?

CASE FILE 6

A group of hikers in the desert comes upon a human skull at the base of a large cliff. They see no other bones nearby. The skull is bleached white from the sun and appears to have been in the desert for a long time. The hikers wonder if the skull is from an old Native American burial site, since there are ancient ruins near where the group is walking. One person uses his boot to turn the skull over and notices that the teeth have metal fillings from dental work. Clearly, this is a modern person who either died out in the desert or whose body was dumped there. How can this person be identified if all that remains is a skull?

in predictable patterns. While bones of the limbs are actively growing, many of them contain developmental features known as growth plates. These are areas of cartilage near the ends of long bones that expand and then gradually change to bone. When a young person's limb bones reach their adult length, the cartilage growth plates seal shut. Based on genetics, the ultimate sizes of the same bones from different individuals will vary, making some people naturally shorter and others taller. If a child is unhealthy, growth may not occur properly, which may leave permanent effects on all body systems, including the skeleton. Lack of exercise, poor nutrition, or an injury to a growth plate may permanently stunt bone growth and development.

Other changes occur in the skeleton when a young person goes through puberty. An adolescent male begins to produce increased levels of the hormone testosterone, which affects his bone development and muscle mass. Male hormones cause men to have bigger joints and more well-defined muscle attachment sites on their bones. For example, adult males typically have a larger jaw that is squared in the front and a more prominent bony brow ridge above their eyes. Most women have a smaller jaw that comes to a single point in front and a smoother forehead area.

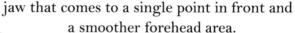

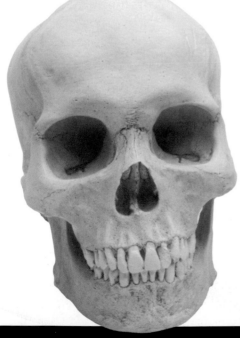

From the shape and size of the jaw, brow, and other skull features in adult skeletons, forensic investigators can often tell a person about their sex. The skull at left is that of a male. The skull at the right belongs to a female.

In a young woman, the production of female hormones, such as estrogen, at puberty leads to wider hips than in males. A mature female pelvis is deeper from front to back and wider from side to side to allow for childbirth. Only after male and female hormones have influenced the body can bones be used by forensic experts to judge a person's sex.

NOT ALL SKELETONS ARE CREATED EQUAL

Physical habits also affect a person's bones. For instance, if a person's job involves heavily using the right arm, the muscle attachment sites on the bones of that arm may become built up or exaggerated. On the other hand, if a person lives a very sedentary lifestyle and has a poor diet, bones may lose part of their mineral content over time. In addition, diseases, injuries, and differences in genetics can all affect bone formation and skeletal health. The result is that not all skeletons are alike, even those from people of the same sex and the same age. The skeleton of a forty-year-old adult man who loads trucks for a living can be quite different from that of a man of the same age who holds a desk job. If that office worker had an injury to his left foot, the bones of that foot may look different from those of his right foot. These differences help forensic scientists identify John or Jane Does from their skeletal remains.

EXPERTS IN BONES

Forensic anthropologists are experts on bone biology and skeletal differences among people. They use clues in bones to estimate a person's age, sex, height, ancestry, and other features related to personal identification. The bones of an unknown individual may be examined for markers of growth. If the skeleton is from an adult, features in the pelvis will be compared to what is known about typical male and female pelvic bones. Long bones are measured to estimate height. Measurements can be taken on the skull of the unidentified person and compared to data that has been gathered from measuring the skulls of known people.

Anything that produces an obvious feature or mark on a bone might be helpful to forensic scientists in establishing a positive identification. Investigators can sometimes tell if a bone was fractured in life and did not heal normally or that a skeletal element did not form properly during development. Pregnancy can leave marks on a woman's pelvic bones that show investigators she may have given birth. Signs of arthritis point to a joint that was injured or used repeatedly for a long time. Loss of bone minerals may suggest old age or poor health.

Forensic scientists can examine these features visually in the bones of a skeleton or view them through X-rays on a fresh or decaying corpse. Specific skeletal information from a John or Jane Doe is then carefully documented. Forensic investigators look for medical records of missing persons to try to match them to the unusual characteristics observed in the unknown skeleton.

ANATOMY OF A TOOTH

Like bones, teeth are extremely durable parts of the body that remain long after other tissues decompose. A tooth has a crown that is visible in the mouth and a root that is anchored in either the upper or lower jaw-bone. Most of a tooth is made up of a bonelike core material called dentin that has a coating of enamel on its exposed surface. Within each tooth is a chamber with blood vessels and nerves that pass through the root. Dentin is living tissue, so the vessels allow nutrients and wastes to be exchanged with the bloodstream. The nerve allows the brain to know when a tooth is damaged by injury or decay. Enamel is the hardest natural material in the body, even stronger than bone. It provides a permanent record of the way some minerals were laid down during tooth development.

Typical patterns of human tooth development are associated with age. Scientists have researched and recorded the usual ages during which each of the baby teeth form and are lost. Much is also known about the timing of permanent tooth development within the jawbone and tooth eruption above the gum. Any growth features that cannot be observed in an open mouth may be seen using X-rays of the jaws. This permits a close look at the stage of crown and root development of teeth still in a child's jawbone and gives an even better estimate of age. By roughly the age of nine, most people have begun to form all the permanent teeth they will ever have within their jaws, though tooth eruption may continue until around the age of twenty-one. Once all permanent teeth are formed, forensic scientists can no longer use tooth development to assess a person's age.

Most people have their teeth examined and X-rayed during regular dental checkups. If so, teeth that are damaged by cavities or broken in an accident will usually be repaired. When dental professionals fill the cavities of decaying teeth, they replace the damaged areas with a variety of artificial substances. These compounds are very durable, and some will last a lifetime. Dentists use different substances in repair, and the parts of teeth that are damaged and restored will vary among patients. As a result, the set of dental fillings a patient receives over time are unique to that person. Since teeth are permanently modified when cavities are filled or when a chipped tooth has an artificial crown, a person's tooth pattern is forever changed by dental work.

Even without dentistry modifications, genetic variations among people make their teeth different. Some people have stronger and thicker enamel than others, tooth crowns can vary in size and shape, and the roots of teeth can differ in their length and curvature. Dental professionals document a patient's teeth in written charts and X-rays. In preparation for braces and other dental procedures, dentists will make casts of an individual's teeth. The casts are often held in storage and become part of a person's dental file. Just like any other medical history, dental records become an important and unique source of information about someone's body. For this reason, tooth anatomy and dental work are valuable in forensic identification.

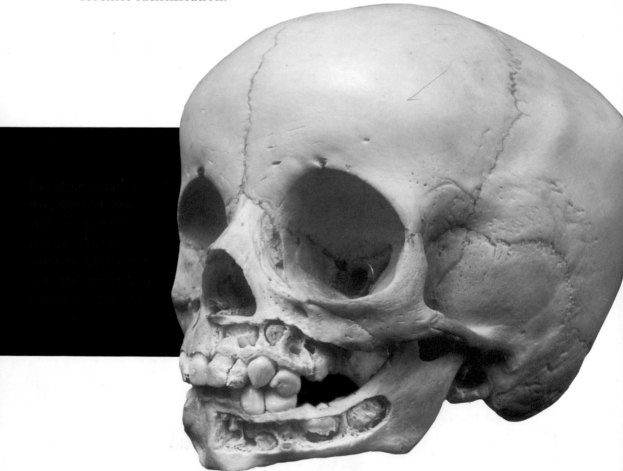

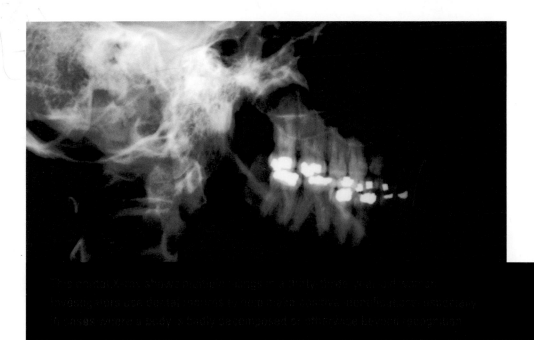

This cranial X-ray shows multiple fillings in a body. Investigators use dental records to confirm a person's identity, especially in cases where a body is badly decomposed or otherwise beyond recognition.

TOOTH TALES

By carefully examining teeth, forensic dentists, known as odontologists, use dental features to aid in identifying the dead. These can include markers of age; health; lifestyle; and perhaps even ancestry, since tooth formation may vary among people of different heritage. A scientific examination of teeth may also reveal aspects of a person's habits, diet, dental hygiene, drug usage, and medical history. For example, people who grind their teeth can wear down the chewing surfaces of the teeth over time. When people of all ages eat lots of sugary foods or do not regularly brush their teeth, bacteria often erode tooth enamel and produce cavities. Illegal drug abuse, especially methamphetamine, can sometimes lead to severe tooth decay and tooth loss known as meth mouth. One or more teeth may be lost in an accident or extracted by a dentist for various reasons. If that occurs, the socket in the jaw will heal over, leaving evidence that a tooth was lost during life, not after death.

When the remains of an unknown person are discovered, forensic odontologists are often involved. Using their expertise, odontologists will compare the teeth of a person in the morgue to dental records collected from any missing individuals who seem a likely match. By looking at the presence and absence of teeth, fillings, crowns, implants, tooth shape, and other characteristics, dental evidence can lead to establishing a positive identification.

Not all people get dental care, however. If odontologists can't locate a dental history for a missing person, they can turn to any X-rays, CT scans, or MRIs of the head that may be available for that person. Sometimes, however, dental evidence may not exist or forensic clues may simply not lead to the right places to look for them.

DURABLE GOODS

The most durable parts of a person's body may not be bones and teeth. Some people have surgical procedures to implant artificial materials into the body. Like dental fillings, these devices may be composed of metal or other materials that do not wear out quickly.

Implanted devices include implements in heart vessels to keep them open, artificial joints, or metal pins and screws in a badly broken bone. A soldier may have metal shrapnel or a bullet fragment in his or her body from an old war wound. Any of these artificial materials may be scattered among skeletal remains or embedded in bones. Through X-ray or autopsy, foreign objects might be discovered in a fresh or decomposing corpse. Any of these items may be helpful to forensic investigators in making a positive identification.

IDENTIFICATION BY THE NUMBERS

Manufacturers of certain types of medical devices are required by law to put serial numbers on their products. If a medical implant or other appliance—whether an artificial joint, a pacemaker, or a breast implant—is recovered with unidentified remains, any serial number on that item might be able to be traced back to the manufacturer. Then, by linking manufacturing records to medical records, the trail should lead back to the patient in which the device was installed. That will, in turn, positively identify that person as the deceased. Other appliances with serial numbers, such as an artificial limb or a hearing aid, also give investigators a very strong lead to follow, even though the devices are not implanted in the body.

PUTTING FLESH ON BONES

Even when a body is badly decomposed and beyond recognition, forensic artists can put a face on the remains. These forensic specialists work with forensic anthropologists, who provide information about the age, sex, and ancestry of the deceased. Given those details, forensic artists use the skull to try to re-create the dead person's appearance.

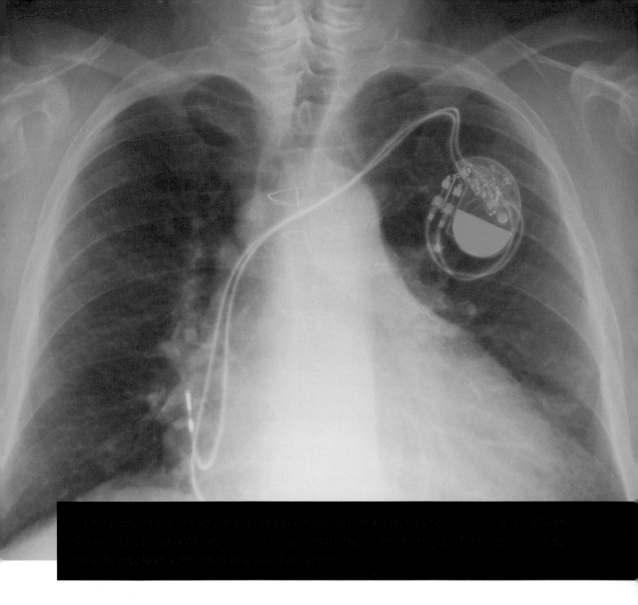

Forensic artists have different methods to restore a facial likeness. One technique involves using the skull as a model and applying clay directly to it for a three-dimensional sculpture. Other methods rely on detailed photographs of the skull from which the artist can create a hand-drawn sketch or images can be uploaded into a computer to manipulate digitally. When a forensic artist makes a clay reconstruction, he or she begins by cutting precise lengths of tissue depth markers that look like pencil erasers. To determine the marker lengths, the artist refers to standards that best match the victim's presumed age, sex, and ancestry. Then the artist applies these markers to specific spots on the skull and carefully sculpts clay over the markers to re-create the victim's face. The artist inserts artificial eyes and adjusts facial features to reflect the victim's ethnicity, if known.

In creating two-dimensional facial reconstructions, artists begin with detailed photographs of the skull, usually taken from several different angles. The forensic artist then sketches by hand or uses computer drawing tools to create a facial likeness. Two-dimensional methods are easier and faster to create than clay models. They can also be altered more easily, if necessary, should more information become known about the victim. In addition, artists can easily and quickly sketch several versions of what John or Jane Doe might look like with different hairstyles, hair color, jewelry, scars, or facial hair.

If a skull still has its teeth, these can be displayed in the reconstruction through parted lips. This may be particularly helpful in identification if the victim had an unusual dental pattern, such as chipped or crooked teeth or a cosmetic implant on a front tooth. If the skull of John or Jane Doe shows that the person had no teeth at the time of death, a forensic artist knows how to adjust the mouth and jaw of the facial likeness to look like a toothless individual. If the skeleton suggests that the dead person was old, the artist can include wrinkles or add gray hair.

Forensic artists can also use a photograph of a missing person and perform an age progression. For example, if a young man ran away from home at the age of fifteen and his family is still looking for him fifteen

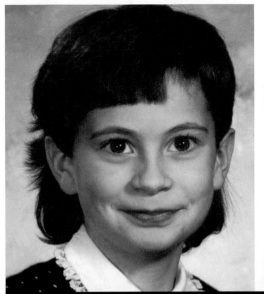

The photo at left shows an eight-year-old girl who is missing. The image at right is a computerized age progression that shows what she might look like fifteen years later, at the age of twenty-three.

years later, a forensic artist may be able to produce an image of that man at the age of thirty from a photograph taken of him at the age of fifteen. If that man lived on the streets to the age of thirty and then died, he may wind up as a John Doe in the morgue. An image of the deceased homeless man could be compared to the artist's age progression of the missing person. Forensic artists can even "erase" facial injuries from unknown victims of accident, suicide, or homicide so that the resulting sketch looks like the person's healthy, living face.

GOING PUBLIC

The goal of any forensic facial reconstruction is to create an image to show the public in the hopes that someone will recognize the deceased. The news account will often contain the details of when and where the remains were found. It also typically includes a description or photographs of any personal effects, such as clothing and jewelry recovered with the deceased. The victim's age and height, based on a skeletal analysis or autopsy, will accompany a photo of the forensic artist's interpretation of the unknown person's face. If someone sees the news story and knows of a missing person who resembles the artist's reconstruction, that person may come forward to help identify the unknown victim.

After recovering bones and clothing in a rolled-up tarp along the side of the road, police took the bundle to the morgue. The forensic pathologist's first step was to X-ray the wrappings and their contents before even opening them. From the bones' growth plates and the developing teeth of the victim, the pathologist immediately realized that the bundle contained the skeletal remains of a young child.

A forensic anthropologist estimated the remains were those of a victim who was about three to five years old at the time of death. Because puberty had not occurred, the anthropologist was unable to tell the pathologist whether the remains were those of a boy or a girl. The amount of decomposition and the decayed clothing suggested that the child had been dead for at least several years. Tattered remnants of a pair of jeans were recovered, as was a size 4T clothing tag, likely from a cotton shirt.

Together, the pathologist and anthropologist noted that the child's remains showed signs of injury and abuse. Some of the bones of the skull and ribs had been broken at or around the time of death. An old fracture of the left arm and other fractures in the ribs were in the process of

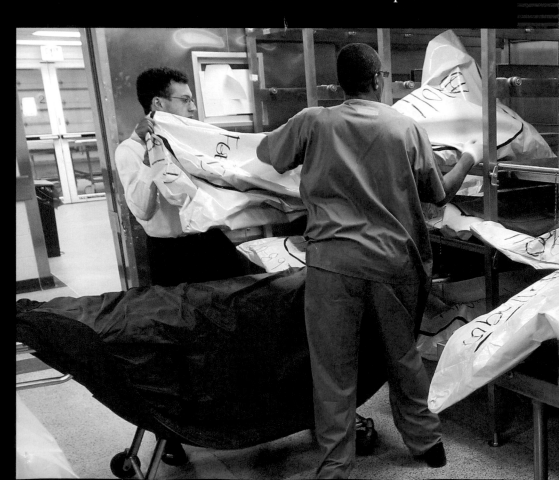

healing at the time the child died. Police investigators in nearby counties were asked to review their cases of missing or abused children between the ages of three and five who had not been seen for several years.

The investigation soon began to center upon a woman who, about five years earlier, had claimed that her four-and-one-half-year-old daughter had been abducted from their yard. At that time, the mother told the police that she never saw the kidnapper and could provide no additional information. The detectives who had questioned the woman years before had always suspected that she knew more than she was admitting. In addition, county hospital records documented a couple of poorly explained injuries suffered by the missing child before her disappearance.

After the body of a young child had been found, the police returned to question the mother again. During questioning the woman confessed that in a fit of rage, she had pushed her little girl down the stairs, unintentionally killing her. In a panicked attempt to cover her crime, the mother wrapped up the little girl, drove to an isolated area, and dumped the body by the side of the road. Presented with the detailed police and forensic evidence, the woman pled guilty to the crimes.

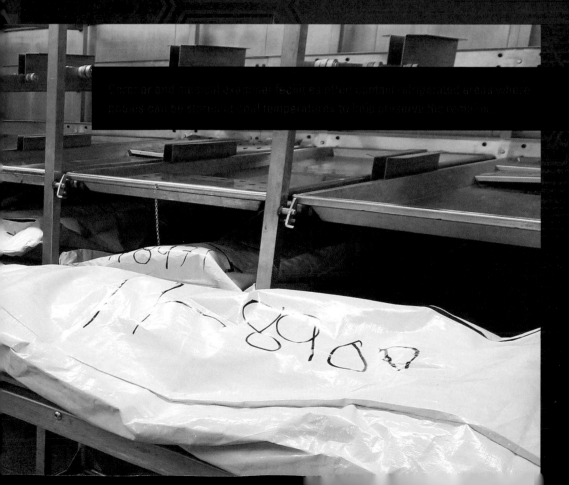

Coroner and medical examiner facilities often contain refrigerated areas where bodies can be stored at cold temperatures to help preserve the remains.

Police were called when hikers discovered a human skull in the desert. Investigators came to the area with dogs trained to locate human remains. They found no additional bones, even after thoroughly searching the cliffs overhead.

The skull was taken to the coroner's office to be studied by a team of forensic specialists. First, an anthropologist measured the skull and compared the data to known standards for sex and ancestry. Based on his analysis, the anthropologist felt confident that the remains were most likely from a Hispanic male. She noted healing sockets in the upper and lower jaw that suggested all four wisdom teeth had been extracted shortly before this man's death The next step included a forensic odontologist, who created a precise chart of all the individual's fillings and took a series of X-rays to document the detailed structure and placement of all teeth. She noted healing sockets in the upper and lower jaw that suggested all four wisdom teeth had been extracted shortly before this man's death. Finally, a forensic artist created a clay reconstruction of the deceased man, and the coroner worked with the media to publish the image throughout the entire region.

Two days after the facial likeness was shown to the public, a woman came forward with information. She said that her older brother had been missing for more than twenty years. The woman told police that the image in the news was very similar to the way her brother had looked the last time she saw him. Her brother was of Hispanic heritage, was thirty-eight years old at the time of his disappearance, and lived alone on the outskirts of the desert. The woman said that her brother often took long hikes into the desert to take photos. Twenty-two years ago, her brother locked up his home, took his camping and photography gear, and was never seen again. Search and rescue teams had used helicopters, all-terrain vehicles, and dogs to scour the surrounding desert at the time, but the man was never found. No one had seen or heard from him again, and the woman had a strong feeling the skull belonged to her brother.

The original missing person's report and the man's dental records were still in storage at the sheriff's office. Back at the morgue, the forensic odontologist was able to compare dental evidence from the victim to the dental records provided by the sheriff. The specific patterns of fillings from the X-rays of the skull at the morgue and the copies of the X-rays in the missing person's file were identical. In addition, the dental record contained a report from an oral surgeon that documented the extraction of the man's four wisdom teeth, only months before he disappeared. Based on the dental comparison, the odontologist was able to confirm that these remains were those of the missing man.

After the 2001 terrorist attacks in New York, search and rescue workers used dogs to look for survivors in the ruins of the twin towers of New York City's World Trade Center. Other dogs known as cadaver dogs, specially trained to detect the scent of human remains, were used to look for deceased victims of the attacks.

CELLS AND MOLECULAR CLUES

LET'S SEE WHAT YOU'RE MADE OF

All organisms—living or dead—are composed of chemicals. In the human body, these chemicals form molecules and cells that, in turn, make up tissues and organs. Each cell nucleus holds DNA, which stores the key instructions for creating and maintaining life. Forensic labs employ scientific experts who use various tests and technologies to analyze body chemistry and DNA as part of the work of identifying remains of unknown persons. Since all body components are made of chemical elements, forensic scientists can perform chemical and molecular analyses on bones, teeth, soft tissues, body fluids, hair, and even individual cells. These types of tests can help establish positive identity whether the remains of an unknown person are in the form of a fresh corpse, decomposing remains, bones, hair, a drop of blood, or a single body cell.

YOU ARE WHAT YOU EAT

The body and its cells are made up of the substances we eat, drink, and breathe. For example, when a person eats or drinks something that is high in calcium, that mineral moves from the digestive tract to the blood. Once in the blood, calcium can be transported around the body

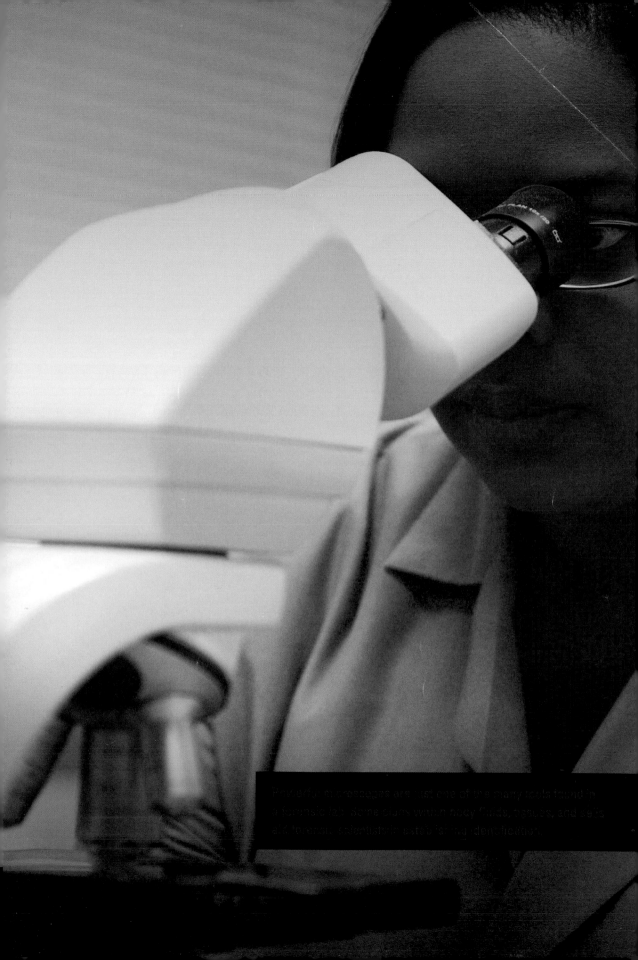

Powerful microscopes are just one of the many tools found in a forensic lab. Some clues which body fluids, tissues, and cells aid forensic scientists in establishing identification.

CASE FILE 7

A frantic man calls 9-1-1 after he receives a package in the mail at his office address. The large envelope contains a T-shirt with what appears to be drops of blood on it. The man tells investigators that his adopted twenty-two-year-old son has been gambling heavily and owes large sums of money to thugs involved in illegal activity. The father states that the night before the package arrived, he received several phone calls from a person who claimed to have kidnapped his son. The caller demanded ransom money and said that he and his accomplices would harm the man's son if the ransom was not paid. Is the substance on the T-shirt human blood? If so, was this shirt taken from the man's son by the kidnappers?

CASE FILE 8

An elderly woman sees a newspaper article about attempts to identify the remains of a young man whose skeleton was found nearly twenty years prior. The issue has been reopened by the state bureau of criminal investigation and its newly formed cold case squad. The newspaper account includes a picture of a facial reconstruction by a forensic artist. The woman thinks the image resembles her nephew, who disappeared about thirty years before. Could the skeletal remains be from her long-lost nephew?

for use wherever it's needed. Any excess amounts are carried to the bones of the skeletal system to be stored for later use. In addition to calcium, bone tissue has many other key elements, such as carbon, oxygen, nitrogen, sulfur, and hydrogen.

No matter where they live, people eat and drink water and foods that contain the local varieties of hydrogen and carbon isotopes (forms of hydrogen and carbon with different numbers of neutrons) and other chemical elements. As people incorporate regional isotopes into their tissues, the isotopes become chemical markers of the local environment. These isotopes tie people to a specific geographic area and function like a chemical fingerprint.

ISOTOPE TESTING

Isotopes in a person's body may help forensic investigators narrow down the geographic area in which someone had recently been living or where that person lived as a child. For example, if the chemical isotopes in the bones of a skeleton do not match the isotopes from the area of discovery, forensic scientists can assume the person was living somewhere else for at least several years prior to death. On the other hand, if isotopes in the teeth of that same skeleton do match the local environment, then the person might have lived in that area when he or she was young and tooth enamel was still forming.

Forensic scientists can also use knowledge gained from the history of the atomic bomb to identify bodies. When atomic bombs explode, they release a radioactive isotope known as carbon-14 into the environment. The first nuclear bombs were tested in the United States during the late 1930s and the early 1940s. As nuclear bomb testing continued into the 1950s and the 1960s, the amount of carbon-14 in Earth's atmosphere increased to levels much higher than before World War II (1939–1945). Atmospheric levels of carbon-14 reached their highest peak around 1970. At this point, international laws began to limit bomb testing, and the amounts of carbon-14 in the atmosphere have been declining ever since.

Before the invention and testing of atomic bombs, plants and animals (including humans) took in carbon dioxide that contained the isotopes carbon-12 and carbon-13. Humans and other creatures living before the atomic age had very little carbon-14 in their tissues. Forensic testing can measure the amount of carbon-14 in human bones and teeth to get an idea of whether a person lived before or after the creation of the atom

The amount of carbon-14 in human teeth and bones can tell a forensic investigator if a person lived before or after the age of nuclear bombs. The photo above shows a nuclear bomb test in Nevada in 1953, an era of intensive bomb testing in the United States.

bomb. People who lived before the age of nuclear bombs will have very little carbon-14 in their skeleton and teeth. Individuals who lived during the 1960s and the 1970s, however, will show the highest levels of carbon-14 in those tissues. Carbon-14 decays very slowly over time, so the amount of carbon-14 in someone's bones or teeth cannot pinpoint exactly when that person lived, but it can provide examiners a clue. It gives them an idea of whether a skeleton needs a more thorough investigation or whether the case more likely represents historic or even prehistoric remains that are not of forensic significance.

BLOOD AND GUTS

Over time, scientists have developed many types of tissue tests that are helpful in forensic identification. Certain protein enzymes are found in the liquid part of blood and other body fluids. Additionally, other types of protein markers are found on tissue cell surfaces. These enzymes and cell markers come in many varieties and are genetically determined, so they are passed from parents to their children. Furthermore, since the proteins made by human cells are part of what makes us different from other animals, scientists have also developed protein tests that can quickly identify whether tissues, including blood, are from a human or from another type of animal.

Even though body fluids and tissue samples can be analyzed for certain genetically determined proteins, these proteins are not unique to a single person. When several different protein markers are examined together, however, matches between tissue types become more probable, but they are not absolute. Scientists may still use these quick tests on tissue and fluid chemical markers in the beginning stages of a forensic investigation. For example, some chemical tests are used to rapidly determine if a substance is actually human blood. If blood or other tissue is confirmed to be human, these rapid protein tests can be followed by an examination of the molecule that stores the recipes for making all body proteins, including those cell markers and enzymes. That molecule is DNA.

BLOOD TYPING

Before DNA testing was developed, forensic scientists relied on blood types to help in human identification. Red blood cells carry genetically inherited markers on their surfaces that scientists use in blood typing. Red cells come in four major varieties known as type A, type B, type AB, and type O. One of the earliest molecular tests used in forensic science was the identification of blood type from remains found at a crime scene. Not only could such a test be performed on a body from which blood was drawn, but it could also be done on isolated blood that was discovered smeared on an object or dripped on a surface.

Blood type is not unique, however, since large numbers of people have each type of blood. In forensic science, blood typing could be used to exclude a person if that individual's blood type was not the same as the unidentified person's. But blood type alone could not be used to positively identify anyone. For instance, if molecular tests showed the blood from an unidentified body or from a blood sample to be type A, all missing persons of any other blood type would be ruled out as a match. But since a fair percentage of people have type A blood, only a loose association between any missing persons known to have type A could be made in that case.

DNA 101

DNA is a hereditary molecule found in the cells of all life-forms on Earth. DNA's structure includes sugars, phosphates, and a series of four specialized molecules, called nucleotides, that are abbreviated as A, T, C, and G. In a similar way that our twenty-six-letter alphabet can be arranged to form all the words, sentences, paragraphs, and chapters in a book, the four specialized molecules in DNA can be arranged to create the unique recipes for all living organisms.

A segment of DNA that codes for a particular recipe is called a gene. Humans have a tremendously large number of genes in common. Between the recipes used by cells to make body proteins are stretches of DNA that don't specifically code for proteins. These stretches of DNA can repeat over and over and are thought to control the timing and the amounts of various proteins that different people make. Scientists discovered that these control areas are highly variable among humans. For this reason, they created DNA tests to focus on these repeated sequences. The variable DNA sequences in these repeat patterns allow forensic testing to create a molecular profile of the unique parts of a person's DNA, often called a DNA fingerprint.

Human cells actually contain two forms of DNA. One form of DNA exists as chromosomes inside the nucleus of a body cell. This type is known as nuclear DNA. When a new individual is formed, one-half of

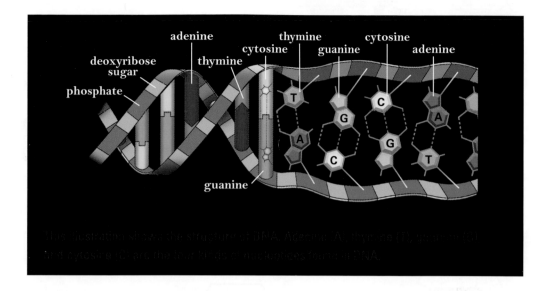

This illustration shows the structure of DNA. Adenine (A), thymine (T), guanine (G), and cytosine (C) are the four kinds of nucleotides found in DNA.

the nuclear DNA is inherited from the egg cell a mother contributes, and the other half is inherited from the sperm cell a father provides. The differences we see among people are due to nuclear DNA variations.

The second kind of DNA in human cells is known as mitochondrial DNA. This type of DNA is not found in the nucleus. It lies in structures inside the cell known as mitochondria. Within complex cells are cellular organs, generally referred to as organelles. Mitochondria are organelles that produce energy for the cell. They are unusual in that they carry their own DNA, different from the DNA inside a cell's nucleus. Mitochondrial DNA is not inherited from both parents. It comes from the mother only.

DNA ANALYSIS

Because human cells have two types of DNA, forensic scientists have developed two types of DNA testing. Tissue cells can be tested to analyze their nuclear DNA, their mitochondrial DNA, or both. Since all cells of the body (with the exception of red blood cells) contain a nucleus, almost any body cell may be used in nuclear DNA testing. Even though red blood cells cannot be used, human blood also contains white blood cells that do possess a nucleus. For this reason, blood is a suitable tissue for nuclear DNA analysis. Nuclear DNA analysis can also be performed on muscle cells, bone cells, skin cells, cells from the lining of the mouth, and even cells present at the root of a single hair. Some tissues are more densely packed with cells, however, and so some tissues yield more nuclear DNA than others.

All cells of the body contain large numbers of mitochondria (including red blood cells), and mitochondrial DNA is more stable in its structure over time than nuclear DNA. For this reason, mitochondrial DNA testing may be easier or better to perform on some tissues than others. The type of tissue recovered, the amount of cells it contains, and the condition of the unidentified remains are all factors in determining which type of DNA test to perform. Forensic scientists must decide which test is best to use in each case.

For a DNA analysis to be useful in a forensic identification, investigators need tissue samples that contain enough DNA to develop a genetic profile, or DNA fingerprint, of the unknown person. Any profile that forensic scientists generate from the deceased will need to be compared to genetic profiles of known individuals. In some cases, these comparisons are made after a suspected or tentative identification has been assumed from other clues. This means the forensic investigators have an idea about the identity of the unknown person based on other evidence, such as a tattoo, a skeletal analysis by a forensic anthropologist, or a driver's license found with the deceased.

To make a DNA comparison, forensic scientists may take the genetic profile obtained from the unidentified body and compare it to DNA from relatives of the person they believe the deceased may be. A DNA sample from a relative is known as a family reference sample. In some cases, the genetic profile from a John or Jane Doe can be compared to an existing DNA profile of the person suspected to be the deceased, if a source of known DNA from that person can be obtained. Sources of DNA from a missing person may be found on that individual's toothbrush, hairbrush, or even from tissue that is in medical storage (such as a blood sample) or from a microscope slide of tissue from a hospital lab. This type of DNA sample is known as a direct sample, since it comes directly from the person who is missing.

DNA DATABASES

National computerized databases of DNA profiles for missing persons, criminals, and other individuals are a key part of human identification. The Combined DNA Index System (CODIS) is a national DNA database that is managed by the FBI. DNA obtained from an unidentified body can be put into the CODIS database, which will compare the profile to others stored in its computerized system. CODIS does not require investigators to have a presumptive identification for a John or Jane Doe.

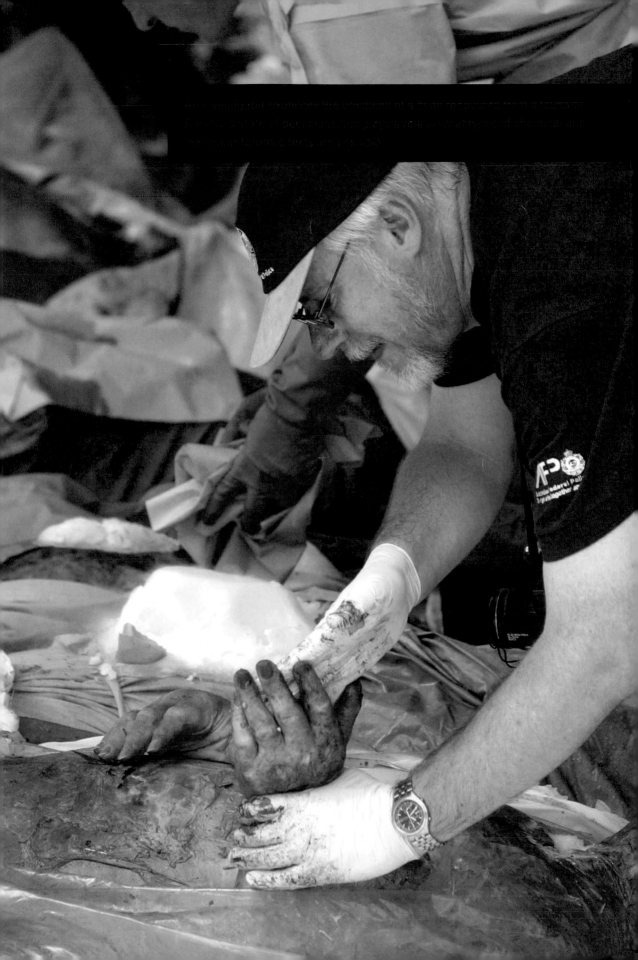

An investigator examines the condition of a body recovered from a tsunami. A victim's state of decomposition plays a role in what types of chemical and physical forensic tests are possible.

The system can compare DNA from any unknown person to all of the database's DNA profiles from missing persons. These profiles are usually submitted by family members of the missing. Even in a case where law enforcement investigators have no idea who a John or Jane Doe is, CODIS might provide what is known as a "cold hit," linking the unidentified person to DNA of someone in the database.

PROS AND CONS

Nuclear DNA is useful because it can be compared to any blood relative on either the mother's or father's side of a victim's family, including the victim's parents themselves. On the other hand, this type of DNA degrades over time, so old tissue samples, such as from skeletal remains that have been in the environment a long time, may contain very little nuclear DNA. For this reason, scientists have developed methods to copy small samples of DNA from a person's cells and make more of the DNA for testing. But when there are very small samples of old and degraded

DNA, making extra copies is often not successful in generating a good nuclear DNA profile.

In addition, the best nuclear DNA comparisons require relatives from both sides of a victim's family. Multiple DNA family reference samples may not always be easy to obtain. Regardless, nuclear DNA is unique to each and every person, with the exception of identical twins, so it is the best molecular source of absolute identification.

Mitochondrial DNA is a much smaller molecule that is more stable over time and does not decompose as easily as nuclear DNA. The chances of getting mitochondrial DNA from bones and teeth that have been in the environment for a while are much greater than obtaining a nuclear DNA profile. In addition, each cell in the body has a huge number of mitochondria, so investigators usually have a greater chance of generating a mitochondrial DNA profile from a tissue sample, even if it is old or degraded. All the same, mitochondrial DNA is not a unique source of information, since mitochondrial DNA is common to all individuals who have descended from the same maternal line.

Because a person receives mitochondria only from his or her mother, the mitochondrial DNA from an unidentified person can only be compared to mitochondrial DNA from siblings that share the same mother, from the mother herself, or from blood relatives in the mother's family. A mitochondrial profile from a John or Jane Doe cannot be compared to the father of the suspected deceased person or anyone linked only from the paternal bloodline. DNA analysts may have to use both nuclear and mitochondrial testing in a forensic case. They will always look at as many features in the DNA profile as possible to make an identification.

Despite some limits of DNA testing, it has revolutionized forensic science. DNA analysis can be very helpful in criminal investigations, and it has become the gold standard in the identification of unknown persons. So far, DNA analysis is the most sophisticated and definite scientific way to positively identify a John or Jane Doe. The odds of two people sharing the same nuclear DNA profile (other than identical twins) are incredibly small—less than one chance out of a quadrillion people (that's a thousand million million). External, dental, and skeletal features are still quite commonly accepted means of identification, as are implanted medical devices. But no matter what other kinds of forensic examination and testing have been performed on an unidentified body, the positive association of two DNA profiles is accepted to be the most definite form of forensic identification.

CLOSING THE CASE

After the mail delivery of a T-shirt with apparent blood stains on it, a worried father called police. His twenty-two-year-old adopted son was missing, and phone calls the man had received the night before pointed to a possible kidnapping. The man knew his son had a gambling problem and was worried that if a ransom was not paid, his son would be killed. When officers arrived on the scene, one of the patrol officers rushed the package containing the T-shirt to the city's forensic laboratory. A forensic scientist closely examined the T-shirt material to study the stains and to look for hairs and other traces of evidence. A rapid enzyme test confirmed that the substance was blood. Then the blood-stain was tested for protein markers. This analysis revealed the blood was from a human and not from any other animal. The blood was type AB, which is rare in the general population. It matched the blood type of the missing man, according to his father.

Police were immediately notified of this information, which prompted a race against time to find out to whom the blood belonged and where the missing man was being held. While officers were running

A forensic scientist examines clothing for evidence. Hairs, blood, and other body fluids may yield DNA that can be used to create a genetic fingerprint of the scene's victim, perpetrator, or both.

Forensic specialists use many tools to gather evidence. Tape can be used to lift fibers and other material from fabric.

down all possible clues to help locate the victim, forensic scientists continued testing physical evidence. The forensic DNA analyst needed to find out whether the blood on the shirt was from the kidnapping victim. She notified police that they would need DNA from a family member so that they could compare it to the DNA profile they hoped to pull out of the blood on the shirt. Police officers asked the father for a DNA sample, but the man reminded them that his son had been adopted. He knew of no blood relatives from which DNA could be obtained. Instead, crime scene investigators went to the young man's apartment, where they gathered personal items from his bathroom. They took his toothbrush and his favorite baseball cap, hoping the forensic lab could obtain a direct DNA sample from one of those sources. Forensic scientists immediately began testing the items for the presence of DNA. The forensic lab also analyzed the packing materials and envelope in which the bloody T-shirt was delivered for DNA or other evidence related to the kidnappers.

Nine days after the father called the police, two different DNA profiles emerged from the evidence. The DNA profile from the blood on the shirt was the same as the DNA from the missing man's toothbrush and ball cap. The other profile was not. Investigators put the unknown profile into the FBI's CODIS databank and got a cold hit. This profile belonged to a local ex-convict who was well known to the police for illegal gambling and other crimes. With this information, the special weapons and tactics (SWAT) team closed in on the suspected location of the hostage. After brief and tense negotiations, the criminals were captured and the kidnap victim was freed.

An elderly woman thought the facial reconstruction in a newspaper article looked very much like that of her missing nephew. She called the police cold case squad and told them about her nephew, who had not been seen in about thirty years. The investigating officers started with very little information about the John Doe skeleton that had been found twenty years earlier. The early records contained nothing more than a few crime scene photos, a short police report, and a brief statement from the pathologist. However, they still had the bones of the skeleton, which had been in storage in the coroner's office for twenty years. When the case was reopened, a forensic anthropologist had analyzed the bones, a forensic artist had created the facial reconstruction, and samples of the unknown man's bones and teeth had been submitted to the lab for DNA analysis.

The forensic anthropologist had indicated the victim was most likely a young black male, about eighteen to twenty-five years old at the time of his death, who had stood around 5 feet 10 to 6 feet 1 inches (1.8 to 1.9 meters) tall. The missing man's aunt told police her nephew was twenty years old, African American, and about 6 feet tall (1.8 m) at the time of his disappearance. She thought that her nephew's dental records had been provided to police decades prior, but she no longer remembered the name of his dentist. Investigators agreed that the facial image generated by the forensic artist strongly resembled photos of the young man provided by his aunt.

Based on all the similarities, the cold case team contacted law enforcement officers from the county where the young man had gone missing. After thirty years, that county had very little information about the case in its files. Furthermore, the missing man's parents had died and his only sister was living halfway across the world. So a member of the cold case unit asked the elderly aunt for a DNA sample. Because she was the sister of the missing man's mother, they would all share the same mitochondrial DNA. They had both descended from one woman who would have been the missing man's grandmother. The team compared the aunt's sample to the DNA profile from the decades-old skeleton. The two samples gave identical mitochondrial DNA profiles. After thirty years, with the help of forensic science, a woman's missing nephew was at last positively identified. The details of his death remained a mystery, but his remaining family members were notified that he was, in fact, dead. His skeleton was buried next to the graves of his parents.

EPILOGUE

In the late 1800s, the victims of serial killer Jack the Ripper in London, England, were identified only because their friends and family members were able to view the bodies and confirm their identities. The science of human identification has changed greatly since that time. Originally, the sole method for identifying the body of an unknown person was to look at external physical features. In the twenty-first century, such surface evidence is still commonly used, but decomposition prevents positive identification in many cases.

Techniques of examining dead bodies have evolved as new technologies have developed. As you read this book, networked computers across the country are examining and analyzing fingerprints for possible matches. Forensic investigators are comparing the photographs of missing and unidentified persons. They are working to match X-rays, CT scans, and MRIs between hospital records of missing persons and the unknown dead. Forensic anthropologists are looking at bones to provide evidence of a person's identity, and odontologists are comparing dental charts and X-rays between individuals. Somewhere a forensic artist is putting clay on a skull or uploading photographs for a computer facial reconstruction. In labs, scientists are looking through microscopes to

find cells and samples of body substances are being taken for analysis. Laboratory equipment is generating the DNA profiles that will allow forensic scientists to compare the molecules of one person to another.

These activities are used in morgues and laboratories of major cities around the world in the quest to put names and faces on John and Jane Does. This is because each day, unidentified remains are found. Isolated bodies are discovered lying in cornfields, in forests, in alleyways, and at truck stops. In Guatemala, Bosnia, the Sudan, and other war-torn places around the world, mass graves are being excavated to attempt to identify those buried in them.

NAMUS.GOV

In the United States, a government-sponsored computer network called the National Missing and Unidentified Persons System (NamUs) has two linked databases of information. On one side of the system, families and law enforcement officers upload the records of missing persons, including

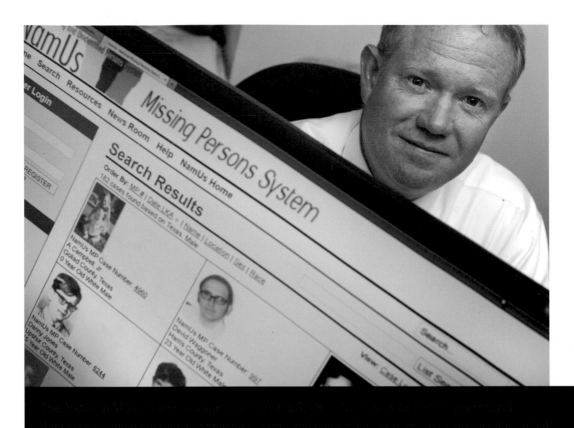

The National Missing and Unidentified Persons System (NamUs) is an online, searchable database for investigating and solving missing and unidentified person cases around the United States. It was launched in 2009 and has helped resolve more than one hundred cases so far.

dental charts, available fingerprint records, and DNA profiles. Another side of the system contains information from coroners and medical examiners taken from unidentified bodies throughout the country. For the first time in history, these records are accessible by the public. Family members can search the NamUs.gov system to see if their loved one fits the characteristics of an unknown person from anywhere in the country. Death investigators can use the system to try to find missing persons whose features may match remains they hold in the morgue. This newly developed forensic tool has the potential to solve many cold cases and will be invaluable to the science of human identification as time goes on.

We can only guess what else the future holds to aid forensic identification. Meanwhile, the dedicated work of scientists and investigators will continue, and the development of new technologies will evolve. This combination of human effort and new tools holds the potential to dramatically decrease the number of John and Jane Does and allows forensic experts to finally restore these people a long-awaited name.

SELECTED BIBLIOGRAPHY

Brenner, John C. *Forensic Science: An Illustrated Dictionary.* Boca Raton, FL: CRC Press, 2004. (Contains some graphic images.)

Eckert, William G., ed. *Introduction to Forensic Sciences.* Boca Raton, FL: CRC Press, 1997.

Evans, Colin. *The Casebook of Forensic Detection: How Science Solved 100 of the World's Most Baffling Crimes.* New York: John Wiley & Sons, 1996.

James, Stuart H., and Jon J. Nordby, eds. *Forensic Science: An Introduction to Scientific and Investigative Techniques.* Boca Raton, FL: CRC Press, 2005.

Kurland, Michael. *How to Solve a Murder: The Forensic Handbook.* New York: McMillan, 1995.

Platt, Richard. *Forensics.* Boston: Kingfisher, 2005.

Rathbun, Ted A., and Jane E. Buikstra. *Human Identification: Case Studies in Forensic Anthropology.* Springfield, IL: Charles C Thomas, 1984.

Reichs, Kathleen J., ed. *Forensic Osteology: Advances in the Identification of Human Remains.* Springfield, IL: Charles C Thomas, 1998.

Ribowsky, Shiya, and Tom Shachtman. *Dead Center: Behind the Scenes at the World's Largest Medical Examiner's Office.* New York: HarperCollins, 2006.

Saferstein, Richard. *Criminalistics: An Introduction to Forensic Science.* Upper Saddle River, NJ: Pearson, 2004.

Siegel, Jay A., and Kathy Mirakovits. *Forensic Science: The Basics.* Boca Raton, FL: CRC Press, 2010. (Contains some graphic images.)

Stimson, Paul G., and Curtis A. Mertz, eds. *Forensic Dentistry.* Boca Raton, FL: CRC Press, 1997.

Taylor, Karen T. *Forensic Art and Illustration.* Boca Raton, FL: CRC Press, 2001.

Thompson, Tim, and Sue Black, eds. *Forensic Human Identification: An Introduction.* Boca Raton, FL: CRC Press, 2007.

Ubelaker, Douglas, and Henry Scammell. *Bones: A Forensic Detective's Casebook.* New York: HarperCollins, 1992.

Walton, Richard H. *Cold Case Homicides: Practical Investigative Techniques.* Boca Raton, FL: CRC Press, 2006.

Winston, Robert. *What Makes Me Me?* New York: DK Publishing, 2004.

FOR FURTHER INFORMATION

Cooper, Christopher. *Forensic Science.* New York: DK Publishing, 2008.

DNA
http://www.dnai.org/d/
Find out more about DNA fingerprinting at this informative website.

The FBI—Federal Bureau of Investigation
http://www.fbi.gov/fun-games/kids/kids-about
The FBI has an accessible site for young people to learn more about the history of the FBI, how it works, and how agents carry out investigations. The site also includes fun games and quizzes.

Fridell, Ron. *Forensic Science.* Minneapolis: Lerner Publications Company, 2007.

"How Fingerprinting Works"
http://science.howstuffworks.com/fingerprinting.htm
This page on the How Stuff Works site gives great basic information about fingerprinting along with a related forensics image gallery.

"How Forensic Dentistry Works"
http://science.howstuffworks.com/forensic-dentistry.htm
This page on the How Stuff Works site offers solid information about forensic odontology along with related forensic photos and videos.

Lucent Books. *Crime Scene Investigations* series. Farmington Hills, MI: Lucent, 2008–2010.

McClafferty, Carla Killough. *The Many Faces of George Washington: Remaking a Presidential Icon.* Minneapolis: Carolrhoda Books, 2011.

Murray, Elizabeth A. *Death: Corpses, Cadavers, and Other Grave Matters.* Minneapolis: Twenty-First Century Books, 2010.

Silverstein, Alvin, Virginia Silverstein, and Laura Silverstein Nunn. *DNA.* Minneapolis: Twenty-First Century Books, 2009.

Smithsonian National Museum of Natural History—Forensic Anthropology
http://anthropology.si.edu/writteninbone/forensic_anthro.html
This website offers great information on how to become a forensic anthropologist and discusses forensic work at the Smithsonian Institution. The site provides fascinating case files of real-life forensic cases, discusses how forensic specialists create facial reconstructions, and has many high-quality photos.

Walker, Sally. *Their Skeletons Speak: Kennewick Man and the Paleoamerican World.* Minneapolis: Carolrhoda Books, 2012.

———. *Written in Bone: Buried Lives of Jamestown and Colonial Maryland.* Minneapolis: Carolrhoda Books, 2009.

INDEX

PHOTO ACKNOWLEDGMENTS

The images in this book are used with the permission of: © iStockphoto.com/ Mark Trost, (fingerprint background); © iStockphoto.com/Roman Okopny, (technology background), (hexagon abstraction background); © Donald Weber/VII/CORBIS, pp. 4–5; © Michael Conroy/AP/CORBIS, p. 7; © Medicimage, LTD/Visuals Unlimited, Inc., p. 9; © Beowulf Sheehan/ Photolibrary/Getty Images, p. 10; © Julian Abram Wainwright/epa/CORBIS, p. 11; PacificCoastNews/Newscom, p. 13; AP Photo/Branson Tri-Lakes Daily News, T. Rob Brown, pp. 14–15; © Charles O'Rear/CORBIS, p. 17; © Bavaria/ Taxi/Getty Images, pp. 18–19; © Laura Westlund/Independent Picture Service, pp. 21, 57; Jim Mahoney/Dallas Morning News, p. 23; © Dr. Gladden Willis/Visuals Unlimited, Inc., p. 24; © Ted Kinsman/Photo Researchers, Inc., p. 26; © Jf123/Dreamstime.com, p. 27 (left); © Dan Ionut Popescu/ Dreamstime.com, p. 27 (center); © Ffikretow/Dreamstime.com, p. 27 (right); © Johan Ordonez/AFP/Getty Images, p. 29; © James L. Castner/Visuals Unlimited, Inc., p. 31; © Marc Abel/Photonica/Getty Images, p. 33; © Living Art Enterprises, LLC/Photo Researchers, Inc., pp. 34–35; © Robert Marlen/ CORBIS, p. 37; © Ralph Hutchings/Visuals Unlimited, Inc, p. 40; Scott Camazine/Newscom, p. 41; © Kallista Images/Getty Images, p. 43; © Tom Murray/Myrtle Beach Sun News/MCT via Getty Images, p. 44; AP Photo, p. 45; © Jeff Kowalsky/Bloomberg via Getty Images, pp. 46–47; © Marcos Townsend/AFP/Getty Images, p. 49; Mike Brown/The Commercial Appeal/Landov, p. 51; © Digital Vision/Photodisc/Getty Images, p. 54; © Adrees Latif/Reuters/CORBIS, p. 59; © SIU/Visuals Unlimited, Inc., p. 60; AP Photo/Steve Helber, p. 62; © Stegerphoto/Peter Arnold/Getty Images, p. 63; © English School/The Bridgeman Art Library/Getty Images, p. 66; © Linda Davidson/The Washington Post via Getty Images, p. 67.

Front cover: © Ulises Rodriguez/epa/CORBIS; © iStockphoto.com/Mark Trost, (fingerprint background); © iStockphoto.com/Roman Okopny, (technology background).

ABOUT THE AUTHOR

Dr. Elizabeth A. Murray has been an educator and a forensic scientist for more than twenty-five years. Her primary teaching focus is human anatomy and physiology and forensic science. She is one of only about seventy anthropologists certified as an expert by the American Board of Forensic Anthropology. Dr. Murray was scientific consultant and on-camera personality for the miniseries *Skeleton Crew* for the National Geographic Channel and a regular cast member on the Discovery Health Channel series *Skeleton Stories*. She has written and delivered a thirty-six-lecture series, *Trails of Evidence: How Forensic Science Works*, produced on DVD by the Teaching Company's the Great Courses. Dr. Murray is also the author of *Death: Corpses, Cadavers, and Other Grave Matters* for juvenile readers.